More Praise for *The Creativity Leap*

"For any of us who feel forced to choose between our creative and analytic selves, this book is a gift, a balm, and an inspiration. Natalie's unique approach to rigor and wonder makes her a wise and relatable coach for building creative competency exactly where we are."
—**Amy Whitaker, author of *Art Thinking***

"In *The Creativity Leap*, Natalie Nixon seamlessly weaves together stories from her personal history with deep insights born from her research to expand on the definition of a 'creative type.' This book offers a new paradigm to those who desire more expansive thinking, imaginative outcomes, and game-changing results for themselves and their organizations."
—**Valerie Jacobs, Chief Insight and Innovation Officer, LPK**

"*The Creativity Leap* is wondrous in its deft blending of insights from sources as different as jazz musicians and GE Healthcare to shed new light on the process of true innovation. Nixon is rigorous in laying out a practical approach that should convince even the most analytic reader of the business value of creativity."
—**Derek Newberry, Behavior and Culture Specialist,**
  Boston Consulting Group

"In her book *The Creativity Leap*, Nixon invites us to bring our whole selves to work and to create with curiosity, improvisation, and intuition. Leaders that want to take the professional development of their team personally and see greater innovation in their organizations should read this book."
—**Erica Keswin, Bestselling author of *Bring Your Human to Work***

"Through insightful stories from her life and innovators across every field, Natalie Nixon shows us how we can build practices that enhance our innate creative competency and provides a valuable reframe on the nature of creativity as the dynamic tension between wonder and rigor. A must-read."
—**Sarah Brooks, Design Director, IBM**

"Imagine a world where creativity is exponentially magnified. *The Creativity Leap* applies methods and insights for creativity in clear, understandable language. Natalie Nixon is a master teacher and has introduced me to that world."
—Stephen Spinelli Jr., PhD, President, Babson College

"With this long overdue book, Natalie delves deep into skills and perspectives necessary for success in a disrupted and dynamic world. For anyone with a desire to construct artful, impact-driving solutions people choose to lean in to, *The Creativity Leap* is a must."
—Esther Franklin, Executive Vice President, Managing Director, Global Strategy and Cultural Fluency, Spark Foundry

"*The Creativity Leap* quickly gets below the buzzwords of innovation to help leaders develop the necessary practices to uncover growth opportunities unleashing new customer and business value."
—Saul Kaplan, founder and Chief Catalyst, Business Innovation Factory

"In *The Creativity Leap*, Natalie Nixon does something brilliant and heretical—she declares that creativity is a teachable phenomenon. Nixon describes creativity as equal parts structure and looseness, focus and ambiguity, rules and no rules, guiding us to an understanding of this most critical ability and daring to suggest that we all have it in us."
—Alan Greenberger, Distinguished Teaching Professor, Drexel University

"We know that creativity is key to success in business, yet few companies actively encourage it, and few individuals in the corporate world really know how to develop it. *The Creativity Leap* is a guide through the process, citing current examples of it in practice and the benefits it brings to individuals and corporations alike."
—Sass Brown, eco-fashion writer

THE CREATIVITY LEAP

THE CREATIVITY LEAP

UNLEASH CURIOSITY, IMPROVISATION, AND INTUITION AT WORK

NATALIE NIXON

Berrett–Koehler Publishers, Inc.

Berrett-Koehler Publishers, Inc.
1333 Broadway, Suite 1000
Oakland, CA 94612-1921
Tel: (510) 817-2277
Fax: (510) 817-2278
www.bkconnection.com

ORDERING INFORMATION
Quantity sales. Special discounts are available on quantity purchases by corporations, associations, and others. For details, contact the "Special Sales Department" at the Berrett-Koehler address above.

Individual sales. Berrett-Koehler publications are available through most bookstores. They can also be ordered directly from Berrett-Koehler: Tel: (800) 929-2929; Fax: (802) 864-7626; www.bkconnection.com.

Orders for college textbook/course adoption use. Please contact Berrett-Koehler: Tel: (800) 929-2929; Fax: (802) 864-7626.

Distributed to the U.S. trade and internationally by Penguin Random House Publisher Services.

Berrett-Koehler and the BK logo are registered trademarks of Berrett-Koehler Publishers, Inc.

Printed in the United States of America

Berrett-Koehler books are printed on long-lasting acid-free paper. When it is available, we choose paper that has been manufactured by environmentally responsible processes. These may include using trees grown in sustainable forests, incorporating recycled paper, minimizing chlorine in bleaching, or recycling the energy produced at the paper mill.

Library of Congress Cataloging-in-Publication Data
Names: Nixon, Natalie W., author.
Title: The creativity leap : unleash curiosity, improvisation, and intuition at work / Natalie Nixon.
Description: First edition. | Oakland, CA : Berrett-Koehler Publishers, Inc., [2020] | Includes bibliographical references and index.
Identifiers: LCCN 2019057689 | ISBN 9781523088256 (paperback) | ISBN 9781523088263 (pdf) | ISBN 9781523088270 (epub)
Subjects: LCSH: Creative ability in business. | Creative thinking. | New products.
Classification: LCC HD53 .N5449 2020 | DDC 650.1—dc23
LC record available at https://lccn.loc.gov/2019057689

First Edition

26 25 24 23 22   10 9 8 7 6 5 4

Book producer: Linda Jupiter Productions; *Text designer:* Kim Scott, Bumpy Design; *Cover designer:* Irene Morris, Morris Design; *Interior illustrator:* Pixel Parlor; *Copy editor:* Elissa Rabellino; *Proofreader:* Mary Kanable; *Indexer:* Pamela Erwin

To John, for being my steadfast source of encouragement through the writing of this book.

And for your daily supply of wonder—and rigor. ✪

Inspiration exists, but it has to find you working.

—Pablo Picasso

CONTENTS

INTRODUCTION

WHAT IS A LEAP?

If you've ever made a running leap, then you are aware that there are several things at work. First, there is vision. You must have your eyes on a prize, somewhere off in the not too far distance. That prize is close enough to be almost within your reach. Second, you have to leap versus just walk or even run to that desired prize, because there is some barrier or impediment that you need to span. Third, leaps often require a running start. A kinesthetic, active motion is needed for you to gather momentum and propel yourself forward. Fourth, leaping requires that you suspend judgment. After doing all the analysis, gauging, and estimating of what it will take to make that leap, faith and intuition must take over. And fifth, leaping only moves you forward. It is impossible to leap backward. You can fall backward, but you cannot leap backward. Leaping requires exorbitant amounts of energy and trust in the unknown—and it always propels us into new territory.

WHY CREATIVITY LEAPS MATTER

Like a physical leap, a creativity leap is essential for crossing boundaries; it is also an active, dynamic process that honors intuition. Creativity leaps are needed to bridge the gap between the churn of work and the highly sought-after prize called innovation. This holds true on both the individual and organizational levels. Creativity leaps matter because creativity is the engine for innovation.

How often have you heard people mutter, "Oh, I'm not a creative type"? Perhaps you've thought this yourself. This is a falsehood because to be human is to be hardwired to be creative. To be a phenomenal lawyer, manager, doctor, engineer, or plumber requires immense amounts of creativity. Yet our educational system teaches out creativity, and our boardrooms reference it as an afterthought. This is why so many people who are pursuing innovation fail to actually innovate. They expect to generate the new and the novel via systems, structures, and processes that do not honor the uniquely human creative impulse.

Sadly, creativity has been ghettoized and siloed in the arts. This is not fair to artists, and it isn't beneficial to our society at large. People's quality of life is at stake. Employees are experiencing a slow death in their office cubicles, while students are made to sit quietly and absorb massive amounts of information passively in classrooms still modeled after schooling in an agricultural economy. Currently, we have a tech crush. We are obsessed with big data, artificial intelligence, and virtual reality while forgetting that humans are at the beginning and end of all those data points. We are forgetting that creativity is the nonnegotiable ingredient in developing the most amazing tech app, healing the sick, and leading dynamic enterprises.

We live in a complex world where there are many shades of gray. Navigating this uncertain and ambiguous world is not easy. But it doesn't have to be so complicated, either. Let me explain. The important thing to note here is that complication and complexity are not synonyms; they are two distinct concepts.

Complication is change that is difficult to control, yet ultimately that control is within our reach. By definition, complication has clear entry and exit points. You can find your way out of a complicated mess. Take, for example, the internal machinations of a wristwatch, the navigation screen in the cockpit of an airplane, and the electrical wiring infrastructure throughout the United States—these are all examples of complicated systems. If we zoom out to the 30,000-foot level, we can identify an underlying order and logic. Complicated systems have patterns that we can detect, and their conundrums can be resolved with the help of experts. They are predictive.

Complex systems, on the other hand, do not have obvious entry and exit points. Complexity abounds in our lives. Our brains are complex systems full of diverging and converging neural pathways. The American health care system is also extremely complex, confounding patients every day in their attempts to navigate it and get clear answers on what ails them and even how to pay their bills. We are embedded in complex systems today that are not predictive, are hard to manage, and require perspective and regular experimentation.

Complexity requires expansive perspective and multiple vantage points in order to see a full and complete picture. Imagine you are a tourist in Midtown Manhattan, standing on a busy street corner. Consider the sensory overload coming at you: the sounds of car horns honking, music from the jumbo screens, crowds of people walking rapidly past you, the smells from food trucks, and signage on the entry staircase to eight different subway lines can be overwhelming. It is only if you were able to see your location from the window of a nearby skyscraper that a pattern would emerge. And perhaps even more clarity would result if you saw the entire island of Manhattan from the vantage point of a helicopter. Complex systems typically require a level of zooming out beyond discrete amounts of time and scope to see the full picture.

Complex systems are self-organizing, adaptive, and emergent. This is one of the reasons why the more diverse skills you
bring into play to solve a complex problem, the more likely
you are to solve that problem. While control is a feasible goal
in complication, that is not the case in complexity. If control
is your goal, then you will be deeply frustrated when facing a
complex problem.

The jazz bassist Charles Mingus said, "Making the simple
complicated is commonplace; making the complicated simple,
awesomely simple, that's creativity." One outcome of applying
creativity is that it simplifies complicated *and* complex problem-
solving by juxtaposing and recombining previously unexplored
counterparts, objects, or ideas. In fact, the best way to navigate complexity is through creativity. Since creativity itself is a
complex system, the open-ended creative techniques of inquiry,
improvisation, and intuition are most effective. That's why creativity leaps matter; they are the only way to solve the complex
problems of our time and to innovate for the future.

CREATIVITY IS A COMPETENCY

Wonder is our capacity to exercise awe, pause, dream, and ask
audacious blue-sky-thinking questions. Rigor is our capacity
to exercise discipline and deep skills, to pay attention to detail,
and to spend time on task for mastery. Both are necessary for
creativity to thrive. In fact, I define creativity as the ability to
toggle between wonder and rigor in order to solve problems
and deliver novel value. And I see inquiry, improvisation, and
intuition as the practices that increase those capacities.

Creativity is not the domain of only one group of people
in our society. To be human is to be hardwired to be creative.
Anyone can be creative, and anyone can become *more* creative.
As you will see in this book, truly innovative people in any

field—lawyers, plumbers, accountants, designers—regularly practice honing their creative competency. They apply a combination of the 3 I's—inquiry, improvisation, and intuition—to the ways they think through problems and work with others to continually increase their creative competency. I call this the 3iCreativity™ model (see Figure 1). They know that these are the tactical means to achieve creativity.

1. *Inquiry.* Curiosity results from an information gap. You want to know more about something that you currently don't understand. Inquiry triggers the leap that bridges that gap. It is the practice of honing your ability to frame and reframe questions, to use questions as a way of thinking through and processing. Inquiry is the root of wisdom and the precursor of empathy.

2. *Improvisation.* Improvising is about building on ideas within minimal constraints. There is freedom to experiment, but there are also rules and fluid structures that help you to correct course and embrace mistakes. It is a deeply observant and adaptive process. Examples of great improvisation show up in jazz, rap, comedy, sales pitches, and scientific experimentation.

3. *Intuition.* There lies in all of us a visceral, internal wisdom that allows for unconscious pattern recognition and insights for decision-making. Harriet Tubman, Albert Einstein, and Steve Jobs are examples of famous innovators and leaders who relied on and valued their intuition, coupling it with their rational intellect to make decisions.

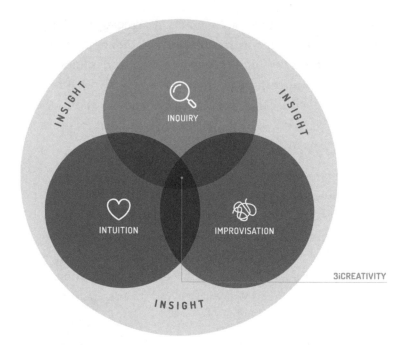

Figure 1. The 3iCreativity model.

These practices require tremendous amounts of trust, courage, and bravery in our times. We must trust that our naive questions will be received well, even if they don't make sense initially. We must have the courage to step out into the unknown, acting in new, untested ways in order to find our footing. We must be brave to follow the nudge in our hearts, that gnawing knowing that may not have any rational basis.

WHY I WROTE THIS BOOK

This book has germinated within me for the past five years. The first seed was planted in 2014 after I gave a TEDx-Philadelphia talk, where I spoke about the ways in which the future of work mimics jazz. This was an outgrowth of my doctoral studies when I applied a jazz heuristic to understand how the Ritz-Carlton Hotel designed experiences for its guests. That talk launched my consulting practice, Figure 8 Thinking, where I help organizations and leaders identify what business they are actually in and apply creativity for transformative business results. The next seed appeared around 2016 as a result of working with entrepreneurs in the start-up world. I observed their continued references to an intuitive nudge to go in one direction over another. I decided to build on that observation by crafting what I called at the time a mini-ethnography of intuitive leadership. I interviewed and observed the ways in which dancers, DJs, and chefs used intuition and pattern recognition to solve problems.

The third seed was planted when I came across Warren Berger's website, A More Beautiful Question. I was infatuated with the simple and compelling model he built around the value of inquiry in innovative companies.

At some point I realized that a practice of these three domains—improvisation, intuition, and inquiry—offers an accessible way for people to tap into their creativity and increase their creativity quotient (CQ). Just as IQ is an indicator of your share of intelligence and EQ connotes your share of empathy, it is also possible to have a share of creativity, or CQ. A creativity quotient is not fixed. It is dynamic and increases as you practice building it and exercising it. Specifically, your share of creativity can increase as you expand your capacity for inquiry, become more willing to improvise, and hone your intuition. Moreover, creativity quotients can be scaled: both individuals and organizations can have a creativity quotient.

For this book, I interviewed 56 people with diverse backgrounds—farming, law, plumbing, architecture, perfumery, medicine, education, and technology, to name a few—between June 2018 and August 2019. I wanted to understand how creativity manifests in their work. I discovered through my conversations with them that a more dynamic and integrative approach is within reach. That approach is the practice of inquiry, improvisation, and intuition detailed in this book.

The Creativity Leap: Unleash Curiosity, Improvisation, and Intuition at Work is a provocation. Its goal is to help you to increase your CQ and your organization's CQ. It encourages you to integrate both wonder and rigor into your daily life in order to produce new and novel products, services, and experiences that deliver greater value to your community and your organization. To this end, you'll gain three major tools from reading this book: catalyzing inquiry, integrating improvisation, and elevating intuition. When you build these three practices into your work on a daily basis, you will discover true creativity—and its output, innovation—beginning to take place.

WHO SHOULD USE THIS BOOK?

At Figure 8 Thinking, I help organizations and leaders become more dynamic versions of themselves and design better experiences for their customers. Too often, I observe clients seeking to innovate without building in the time and processes that encourage creativity in a sustainable way. This is the case whether we are talking about regulated industries like financial services and health care, consumer product goods, or foundations and nonprofit organizations. Organizations may have the rigor down—the meetings, procedures, and rulebooks —but are woefully lacking in the wonder, their capacity to pause and ponder big, audacious questions. As you will learn in this book, rigor cannot be sustained without wonder; and without both capacities, creativity—and innovation—will suffer.

This book is for leaders who suspect there is a more effective and accessible means to go about the goal of innovating. It offers a more dynamic and integrative way to lead, adapt, and innovate, one that allows us the freedom to access our full human selves. This book is for organizations that are struggling with silos, legacy systems, and either a too-big-to-fail attitude or a too-little-to-win complex. It will provoke, invigorate, and share tips on how to make the creativity leap that is necessary to continually adapt in an increasingly complex world.

Many books espouse innovation or creativity, but not enough reveal that the backstage machinations of innovation *are* creativity leaps. This book shares the manifestations of creativity in all its unlikely shapes, forms, and places, and will inspire you to make your own creativity leaps.

WHY ME?

I am a hybrid. I have a background in cultural anthropology and fashion. Both equipped me well, each in its own unique way. My work experience spans being an entrepreneurial hat designer in New York City in the early 1990s; teaching middle-school english; living and working as an expat in Sri Lanka and Portugal making bras and panties for Victoria's Secret; teaching for 16 years as a university professor in fashion management and strategic design; and now consulting as a creativity strategist.

My background in fashion has equipped me with a comprehensive way to approach business strategy. People who have never worked in fashion either dismiss it as frivolous or are intimidated by it. The truth is that only 2 percent of the fashion business is glamorous. The other 98 percent requires robust business acumen. Working in global sourcing—that is, figuring out how to get clothing made with the highest quality, shortest lead time, and lowest cost—taught me supply chain management; logistics; consumer insights; and the value of beauty, aesthetics, and desire in selling products and designing experiences.

I use my anthropology degree in my work every single day. It gives me a worm's-eye view of society and the skill to observe and frame questions. Quantitative approaches and social sciences like economics, sociology, and political science give a bird's-eye view of society. They show us patterns and "the what." But to understand "the why," you must drill down and use techniques like deep observation, contextual inquiry, and interviews. These are all methods that come from anthropology. Ideally, both quantitative and qualitative approaches are used as complements to each other—that is where my hybrid nature shines the brightest.

I spent the last six years of my academic career with a diverse group of colleagues building a Strategic Design MBA program at Thomas Jefferson University in Philadelphia, Pennsylvania. This executive MBA degree applied the studio model for classroom teaching and integrated design thinking throughout its coursework. Our goal in this effort was to creatively disrupt graduate business school education. We were convinced that interweaving human-centered innovation—empathy, proto-typing, and the ability to visualize data—into the ways that working professionals learned strategy was setting them up for success. After I resigned from the university, the program was incorporated into a preexisting, more traditional MBA degree. I am proud of our efforts to formalize a hybrid approach to learning: The impact it had on alumni lives on.

In some ways, this book is a reflection of my own inherent indecisiveness. I never felt comfortable choosing sides by self-identifying as "more analytical" or "more creative." In fact, I now know that a spectrum bounded by these two variables is totally off course. This is because creativity requires analytical rigor, and analysis requires a capacity for wonder to make sense of a conundrum. And as it turns out, a hybrid approach to creativity and innovation that incorporates wonder and rigor is more essential than ever.

MY AUDACIOUS GOAL

Art is seeing the world that does not exist. . . .
Civil rights activists are artists. Athletes are artists.
People who imagine something that is not there.

—Oscar-nominated filmmaker Ava DuVernay

I love this expanded definition of art as "seeing the world that does not exist." As a collective of humans on this earth, we need to piece together a world of work that does not yet exist, one where people show up fully invited to bring their whole selves to their jobs and to create. Currently, this is not the way most people get to work, but it is the optimal way, and it will result in happier employees and customers. My audacious goal is that this book will help us to make the creativity leap over the gap between what is today and the optimal world of work we must build.

CHAPTER 1

CREATE LIKE YOUR LIFE DEPENDS ON IT

WHY CREATIVITY MATTERS

I've been collecting signals on the landscape, indicators that we are increasingly valuing our uniquely human ways of thinking and creating in our business life. One signal comes from the management consultancy Capgemini. In 2015, Capgemini published a report titled "When Digital Disruption Strikes: How Can Incumbents Respond?" It begins with this striking sentence: "Since 2000, 52% of companies in the Fortune 500 have either gone bankrupt, been acquired, or ceased to exist."[1]

The core reason for this failure has been chalked up to an inability to adapt. But let's dig deeper as to why it's hard to adapt. Part of it involves the "too big to fail" assumption and superiority complex that emerge when organizations find themselves at the head of the pack. But where does that mindset come from? It is not enough to say that these firms don't innovate quickly enough. They get complacent and stuck. Michael Forman, chairman and CEO at FS Investments, told me that as organizations get larger and more focused on risk management, they easily fall into what he calls "the tyranny of no." "They solve for 'no' instead of for 'yes.' Solving for 'yes' is the fulcrum of creativity." He observed that the larger reason for why successful companies fail is that they do not cultivate their capacity for human creativity.

A second signal showing up in an unexpected place comes from the World Economic Forum (WEF). In 2016, the WEF predicted that by 2020, creativity would rank as the number 3 job skill. Consider that the WEF had ranked creativity as the number 10 job skill in 2015. What is interesting is that they predicted critical thinking and complex problem-solving would rank first and second by 2020. But guess what? Creativity *requires* critical thinking and complex problem-solving—so we essentially have creativity leading the pack in important job skills for the future of work (see Figure 2).

Yet another sign I've witnessed was in the Showtime hit series *Billions*. Character Wendy Rhoades is among the C-suite of executives at Axe Capital. She counsels the group of intense, testosterone-driven venture capitalists to tune in to their inner voice, learn to meditate, and visualize success. I am increasingly seeing the value of people with backgrounds in the humanities, psychology, and cognitive science in unusual spaces.

Perhaps the biggest signal of all occurred in the summer of 2019. *Business Insider* announced that a convening of leaders of Fortune 100 firms had culminated in an acknowledgment that stakeholder value was as important as shareholder value.[2] While many have a wait-and-see attitude about how these companies will demonstrate through their actions that people (and the planet) matter just as much as profit, it is significant that these leaders spoke this value out loud.

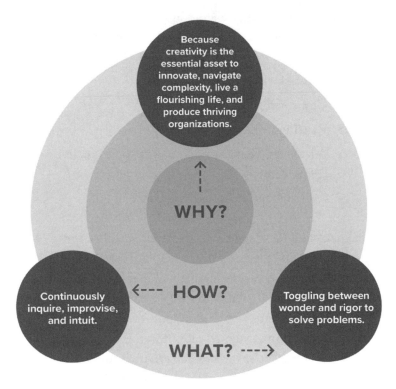

Figure 2. What is creativity?

WHY DO WE DISMISS CREATIVITY?

Research from Steelcase, a furniture design company, presents interesting insights about collaboration at work and creativity.[3] They surveyed 4,500 people in Germany, France, England, Spain, the United States, and Japan. The following were some of the more relevant points regarding creativity:

- 14 percent were not given a chance to express their creativity.
- 55 percent wanted to be more creative in their role.

- Generation Y and Generation Z showed more creative ambition than older workers (60 percent versus 50 percent).

- Creative blocks included these:

  ◆ Uninspiring space (20 percent)

  ◆ Existing workload (36 percent)

  ◆ A lack of guidance or permission to be creative (19 percent)

  ◆ Outdated technology (20 percent)

In spite of all these signals on the landscape, I'm convinced that we don't hear creativity emphasized more in the boardroom because we don't actually understand creativity. I define creativity as our ability to toggle between wonder and rigor to solve problems and produce novel value. While many companies are trying to figure out innovation, most corporate cultures rarely utter the word *creativity*, and there is not a carved-out space in the boardroom for creativity. This goes back to the ways that we have partitioned it off as being only in the domain of the arts, making creativity appear inaccessible and in the realm of the few, not the many. In his 2007 TED Talk, Sir Ken Robinson, well-known adviser on education in the arts, spoke about the decline in creative confidence. He shared how when kindergarten students are asked, "Who wants to be an artist?" the majority of hands fly up. By high school, that cheerful endorsement of the arts as a career path dwindles down to less than a quarter of the students.

Perhaps creativity feels so inaccessible because it can be such an ambiguous process. It is not formulaic. It is complex. That lack of a rote, step-by-step approach can make it really uncomfortable. The arts have become the default space where we identify creativity because artists are required to sit with the ambiguity of not knowing where their creative process will lead them. They commit themselves to wrestling with the discomfort of it all.

LinkedIn produces a podcast about work called *Hello Monday*. In one episode, the actor Laura Linney was interviewed by Jessi Hempel about what makes for good criticism.[4] In it she discussed the value of "sitting with discomfort." As an artist, she has grown to expect this as part of her work in creating a character and collaborating with other actors. I was struck by how much she accepted that discomfort and the ambiguity of it all.

A creativity leap entails our seeing and listening with wonder and rigor in order to sort through the ambiguity and uncertainty of a work process. The awareness that Linney described points to the amount of astute seeing and listening we must do in order to create. It is only through that deep listening and observation that we uncover the finer points that need tuning and realignment.

Fundamentally, the arts teach us how to see things from different perspectives. For example, when you learn how to draw a vase, you must observe not only the solid matter in front of you but all of the context around the vase. An early exercise may be to start with a contour line drawing, only drawing the outline of the object in front of you. By default, you wind up drawing the "negative space." Negative space refers to the in-between bits of color, light, and shadow that begin to take shape in the space outside of the boundary lines of the object. Think of the Rubin's vase optical illusion, also referred to as the figure-ground vase. In this puzzle drawing, you might alternate between seeing either a woman's profile or a vase. It is a classic way of demonstrating that what we see can be amplified, diminished, or crystallized if we not only look at what is obviously in front of us but also shift our focus a bit to what is on the periphery or just beyond. It helps us to question our assumptions about what is, and to see things from varied perspectives.

Julian Harzheim and I met in Shenzhen, China, in 2018, at the European Innovation Academy (EIA), a business accelerator program. It wasn't enough that he was a German studying at Nova University of Lisbon, Portugal, and showing up in Shenzhen with social impact desires. What dazzled me further was the story he shared over a coffee about starting Creative Hub at Nova.

During the first week of business school in Lisbon, one of Julian's professors asked the class, "How many of you believe that creativity will be one of the most important skills in the future?" All hands shot up. When the professor asked this follow-up question, "How many of you believe you are creative?" the majority of students' hands went down. Julian saw a problem—and an opportunity. And so he started Creative Hub with a handful of other MBA students as an experiment, as a platform to bring forward new ideas. One workshop focused on storytelling and was run by graffiti artists. Another event, called the Lemonade Challenge, gave students 20 Euros to come up with better ways to market lemonade.

Julian started Creative Hub with a bit of wonder and dug in with rigor to bring it to fruition. Applying our human capacity for creativity and inventiveness to problem-solving was a game changer for him. It has made a huge impact on his life: "It gave me the confidence to believe in my ideas. It was also a pilot test phase for me to see how I could build a team with only a vision. And nothing else." Today Julian has graduated and works with a start-up in Lisbon whose mission is to end wildfires in Portugal.

These are the benefits of sitting with the discomfort and ambiguity that arise during the creative process. In Julian's case, this push outside of his comfort zone helped him build the muscle of believing in his own ideas. Instead of avoiding the discomfort of uncertainty, he grappled with it. Winston Churchill said, "When you're going through hell, keep going." There is no other, romanticized way around it. This is the rigor of the creative process.

MAKING CREATIVITY ACCESSIBLE

Does your organization have a department of innovation, an innovation lab, or an innovation studio? If it does, that is great, because it indicates a desire to not continue doing things in the ways they have always been done. But going from having an innovation center to having a culture of innovation demands a creativity leap. It requires intentionality and the integration of a new mind-set at all levels of the organization. Otherwise, you have created just one more silo in your company.

People throw around the word *innovation* all the time; sometimes we end up talking around each other without getting to the real definition. What do we mean by innovation? Innovation is invention converted into financial, social, and cultural value. Furthermore, the engine for innovation is creativity. That means that if we truly want to innovate, then we must design systems, processes, and experiences in our work environments that allow us to be creative and catalyze invention.

If all we are doing is setting aside new departments or spaces that we designate as the space in which to innovate, then it is as if we are saying there is a separate time and space to be creative and to be productive. And that just is not so. Creativity is a productivity play. That is why it is essential for business, not just some frilly, extraneous add-on. Taking the leap to build an organization-wide creative capacity is the single best way to continually innovate.

The first step is making creativity a resource that is accessible to all the people in your organization. Defining creativity as a competency consisting of wonder and rigor, and exercised through inquiry, improvisation, and intuition, is one way to democratize it. Viewed from this lens, creativity becomes available to all of us.

Inquiry, or curiosity, is the foundation, because without the ability to ask questions, you cannot be self-reflective; you are stuck. One of the major takeaways I have gotten from Warren Berger's book *A More Beautiful Question* is that asking questions is really a way of thinking.[5]

Improvisation is your ability to be present in the now and to be responsive with those around you. There are rules to improvisation; it is not doing whatever you feel like doing. The beauty and fun of improvising is that you get to stretch and rebound off of minimal structures in order to create something entirely new. Improvisation is all about the remix.

Intuition is that connection between the heart and mind, grounded in your gut. It is unconscious pattern recognition. It is often what fuels us to finally make that creativity leap.

Inquiry, improvisation, and intuition don't need to be followed in any particular formulaic order. Their use is situational, and there is an ebb and flow between them resulting in insights. This is what makes creativity the engine for innovation.

The psychologist Mihaly Csikszentmihalyi defined *flow* as the state during which you are so immersed in an activity that nothing else matters. You are neither aware of the time nor self-conscious. Csikszentmihalyi considers flow as the means to creativity and the secret to happiness. He writes about creativity as moments that make life worth living when there is total flow.

That flow can happen on both the individual and organizational levels, but not until we stop ghettoizing creativity and relegating it to the domain of artists. The false dichotomy of creatives versus noncreatives puts the onus of creativity solely on artists. This isn't fair. To expect that all creative outcomes must stem from artists is a lot to ask—especially given the fact that in the United States we don't set up artists to succeed in terms of funding or real acknowledgment of their contributions to our economy. Instead, we should all share the responsibility of being catalysts for creativity because creativity resides in all of us.

When I began my interview with Jeff Benjamin, the COO at Fitler Club, a full-service urban social club for professionals, he initially said, "I don't view myself as a creative." There goes that qualifier again: "a creative." Let's remove the "a" and just sit with "creative" for a moment. By the middle of our conversation, Jeff made an enlightened remark: "Creativity is as individual as a snowflake. My restaurant managers are my customers. They're my table. I'm waiting on them." And that is where he sees his creative energy surging.

As Jeff came to realize, to be dynamic at anything—as EVP of operations, an attorney, a scientist, an entrepreneur, or a plumber—you must be consistently creative, drawing on your capacity for asking audacious questions, working off script, and following your gut instincts.

CREATIVITY IS HOW WE LEAP FORWARD

Humans are creatures of habit and tend to crave certainty. And when you need to stay in your lane, it may be safe to establish benchmarks that are local and accessible and germane to your industry. But benchmarks are relative boundaries. The broader you need your thinking to be, the broader should be your benchmark.

When I was a professor and developed a strategic design MBA program, I fell in love with the design thinking process. I appreciate it as a problem-solving tool that organizations can apply to produce more customer-centered products and services. In addition to empathy, prototyping, and visualizing data, one of its important hallmarks is lateral thinking. Lateral thinking is the ability to learn from sectors and practices both adjacent to you and far away from the way you typically do business. For example, if you are a tech firm, you might explore theatrical production to learn about project management, or you might intentionally align with an instigator such as BCG Digital Ventures. Lateral thinking opens you up to the opportunity of choosing new benchmarks so that you can make creativity leaps. I realize now that this is what allowed the manufacturing teams I once worked with to innovate old designs and create freshly styled brassieres.

Years ago, I lived in Colombo, Sri Lanka, and then Porto, Portugal, making bras and panties for the Victoria's Secret brand. During this short stint in my career working in apparel fashion sourcing, I learned the logistics and manufacturing side of the fashion business. Working directly on the ground with fabric mills and cut-and-sew factories was an amazing education about production and quality control. A brassiere is a relatively complex object. It consists of more than 30 components, and the ability to deliver consistency in fit and color over multiple sourcing locations is no small feat.

Often, the factories would establish benchmarks, or standards, by gauging what competitors in the same category were doing. Standards were established by looking internally, within the same sector. But consistently, the biggest breakthroughs in design direction came not only from using other apparel or fabric companies as reference points but also from implementing engineering workarounds and ingenious materials selection.

It was when we broke out of our norms and looked laterally to adjacent areas or to totally new realms that inspiration materialized. For example, at the time, laser cutting and 3-D digital printing were relatively new technologies, just being introduced into apparel production. It was remarkable to see the engineers and fashion designers troubleshoot new and interesting ways to develop edging and cutouts from fabric where shrinkage and the fibers' melting points had to be considered.

New benchmarks have been Kevin Bethune's raison d'être as a leader in strategic design. Kevin is the founder and chief creative officer at dreams • design + life, a self-described "think tank that delivers design and innovation services using a human-centered approach." He told me his story of working at Nike after earning his MBA and gradually inching his way into working with the design teams. One of the ways he did this was by regularly contributing to their brainstorm wall and posting exemplars that came from new and different areas. He would ask, "Have we looked *outside* of the Nike walls? What other trends are shaping this space?" At the time, he was not formally trained as a designer. His first degree was in engineering. So his nonexpert perspective added fresh-eyes value to identifying new benchmarks.

Kevin describes creativity as "the opportunity to combine, recombine, disrupt, or creatively destroy existing things and known elements into new and interesting combinations." He certainly had to do this later in his career as cofounder of BCG Digital Ventures, a corporate investment and incubation firm. Kevin and his team convinced start-ups to remove themselves from the safety of their own environment to reorient themselves and learn how to research and collect new insights. Space matters in establishing new benchmarks and navigating complexity. In fact, BCG Digital Ventures experimented with space to the extent that some rooms were in the shape of a hexagon to help people work more fluidly and in truly multidisciplinary ways.

When you are trying to leap into new frontiers as a business, you must identify new landmarks and new benchmarks, and get into a new space to work. When you are trying to break out of the mold, you must be audacious to make that creativity leap into new territory.

CREATIVITY LEAP EXERCISE

FOR YOU
► Become a clumsy student of something. Cultivate a new hobby. Marvel at how good you become at asking questions, improvising, building on mistakes, and intuiting.

FOR YOUR ORGANIZATION
► Build on Kevin Bethune's model: What are the trends and the exemplars outside of your industry that your company should be paying attention to?

CHAPTER 2

FLOW BETWEEN WONDER AND RIGOR

WISDOM BEGINS IN WONDER

My elementary school report cards are littered with comments that are variations of the following: "Natalie is a delight and is making good progress in the second grade. However, she tends to daydream out of the window a bit too much . . . "

I was, and remain, a mighty daydreamer. Daydreams are like a magnetic pull for me. What begins as a glance at a small object blurs into the depths of my mind until I pull myself out of my reverie to go back to the matter at hand. I always feel refreshed when I return back to "normal." The reverie serves as a type of marinating time for my new ideas.

Now I can point to thought leaders on the neuroscience of creativity to defend my propensity to daydream. Daniel Levitin's *The Organized Mind: Thinking Straight in the Age of Information Overload* and Daniel Kahneman's *Thinking, Fast and Slow* demonstrate that innovation happens not during our intentional, laser-focused modes but when we are daydreaming.

These psychologists offer up the science to help us value our intuitive thinking systems that allow ideas to germinate in our dreams.

Daydreaming leads to wonder. Pay attention to how many times you, your colleagues, and your teammates begin a sentence with "I wonder if . . . " or "I wonder what might happen when . . . " Observe what follows those two words, "I wonder . . . " What we begin to wonder about brings us to the precipice of discovery. Therein lies the magic. It is more concerning if you and those around you are *not* starting their sentences with "I wonder . . . " That admittance of ignorance and curiosity is critical. Don't stop yourself or others—follow the bread crumbs to where that wondrous state leads.

Wonder requires a space of doing nothing. This may be a radical proposition in our times of fast-paced, just-in-time expectations. The art of doing nothing requires suspension of assumptions and the ability to wait. Waiting can be nerve-racking. But as discussed in the previous chapter, it is rigorous work to sit with the ambiguity of not knowing and sensing out options. My mom used to advise me, "When you don't yet know what to do, do nothing. Just wait. There are always variables shifting around us."

Sometimes it is the pause, the giving of permission to reflect, that leads to the most important breakthrough moments. Karima Zedan, the director of Internet Essentials at Comcast Corporation, shared the following example with me. Internet Essentials is the arm of Comcast whose mission is to close the digital divide among low-income households and ensure internet access. They partner with nonprofit organizations around the USA. Karima leads a diverse team of people, focusing on research, strategy, and marketing. The value of the pause came into play when she and a team member were debating the interpretation of statistics in a report.

> We went back and forth on an email for a long time, and emotions got heated. We kept pushing against another colleague's interpretation. And then I said to the woman on my team, "Let's take a step back. Is there any possibility that he is right?" We looked a solid five minutes at the work. And my colleague said, "You know what, he is right." The point is, we get emotionally charged about numbers. We get attached, and do not always pause to allow other opinions to emerge. Now, I continually ask, "Is there any way that person is right?"

In this situation, pausing to wonder allowed Karima to step back and gain perspective. It also helped her to connect respectfully to a colleague's at-first-contrary insight. If we are to truly innovate and make creativity leaps, then we must start from a wondrous state, revving up our curiosity and desire to explore.

WONDER AND CREATIVITY

Wonder is the component of creativity that requires awe, audacity, pausing, and asking audacious "What if . . . ?" questions. Complex situations are grand in scale, so they deserve and require the grandiose thinking that wonder inspires. The challenge is that very few of our organizations and work processes allow for wonder. Exploration is cut short by the need for expediency. Rapid-response solutions are rewarded.

The root of the problem lies in our educational systems, even before we have shown up to our first job. Many of us have been taught to be very good at having the one right answer. We are rewarded for connecting the dots and are cautioned not to go outside of the lines. The last time some of us were encouraged to be playful in a learning context was in kindergarten. By the first, second, and third grades we are taught to conform, sit still, and abide by rules. Not that rules aren't important (we will get to those next), but forsaking wonder and the freedom that comes with it, only for structure and order, is not ideal.

Pausing to wonder about something spurs new questions. After all, every sentence beginning with the words "I wonder" necessarily ends with a question mark. Wonder likes to test out new ways of being and doing, rebounding off of the constraints of current knowledge. The only way we get to make a creativity leap in the first place is by starting with wonder. Wonder is the catalyst. Then, rigor propels us forward and helps us to sustain the momentum of the leap.

RIGOR AND RULES

There are several variations of the story about why my mother put me in a Horton technique modern dance class at age four. One version is that she observed how energized I became as a baby when, in my playpen, I would mimic her movements as she exercised. Another version is that I was (and still am) shockingly clumsy. She got me started in dance lessons with the hope that I would acquire some grace and a sense of spatial relations. In any event, I experienced the initial years of studying dance to be full of rigor and rules. Lots of them.

You learn how to dance, to stretch and train your muscles, through repetition. It's hard, sweaty work; it's not sexy. It feels like you will never be able to actually dance and float in the ways the ballerinas and great modern dancers on stage do. This is the part of the process that famed modern dancer and choreographer Twyla Tharp calls "the box." As she has wisely advised, "Before you can think out of the box, you must start with a box." The box is the rules and the rigor. And there is no getting around it.

Leonardo da Vinci is credited for having said, "Every obstacle is destroyed through rigor." Da Vinci was one of the greatest known polymaths in history. We can attribute the

term *Renaissance man* to his developed expertise in paint-
ing, architecture, mathematics, and astronomy. His creativity
was sourced not only through his immense curiosity but also
through the rigor that he applied in order to learn the details
of these wide-ranging fields. These diverse fields could also be
played off of each other, for, as my mother taught us when we
were young, all learning is interconnected.

Statistics are driven by facts and rigor. I'm neighbors with
Sean Forman, the founder of Sports Reference. His unassuming
office is located in the coworking space of a church in the resi-
dential Mount Airy community of Philadelphia. Sean has rock
star stature in the world of sports statistics. Sports Reference
has been featured in the *New York Times*, and the website has
generated millions of page views. When I interviewed Sean, the
work process he described reflects the toggling between wonder
and rigor necessary for problem-solving:

> I work on multiple fronts and edge forward to get to
> a solution that is intuitive to the end user. I have to
> back out and work out new solutions—piecing all that
> together and then managing it. It's not creativity like
> a painting on a wall; it is a living, breathing thing to
> which we add data.

The output of Sean's rigorous process contributes a novel
way for sports fans to consume information about their favorite
teams and players. Working out a better-framed question and
pushing through process require rigor.

In my interview with Brent Sherwood, a space architect
at NASA, he reminded me how we need to rigorously design
the structure and boundaries of our work projects so that we
understand the limits to be pushed. Boundaries, structure,
rules, and limits are essential. They are modalities to help us get
great at our craft.

One of my heroes is Beethoven. There is no way he could have created his century's version of romantic music without having been expert in the classical music of the last century. You cannot break the rules unless you understand the rules. It may lead to someplace new and into new territory.

The journey to becoming an expert requires an inordinate amount of time and focus on minutiae and details, and spending lots of time on task. Without the focus that rigor requires, we would not appreciate the times of wonder—nor would we be able to complete the creativity leap that wonder initiates.

RIGOR AND CREATIVITY

As a little girl in the 1970s, I absolutely loved Donna Summer. I loved her big, soft hair; her pretty, shiny red lips; her doe eyes; and her fearless voice. Even as a seven-year-old, I knew I had to have that cassette tape. So, some 40 years later when my husband gifted me tickets to see the Donna Summer musical, *Summer*, produced posthumously at the Lunt-Fontanne Theater in New York City, it was magic. The dazzling set design, sparkling lights, stunning choreography, and bold singing transported me. In 1977, I was enraptured with the wonder of it all. By 2017, I could also appreciate the rigor of it all.

If wonder is the equivalent of experiencing opening night of a marvelous theatrical experience, then rigor is all of the backstage machinations. It's the cable cords holding the velvet curtains in place, the dark hallways and underground tunnels, and the rafters holding lights engineered to create surreal effects. It is the incessant practice that the actors, dancers, and singers must engage in all the way up to opening night.

If we romanticize creativity as a mystical, magical process only accessible to a select few, then we miss the point. Creativity is not something you pull willy-nilly from your armpit. Rigor is that essential feature of creativity that anchors the wonder; puts guardrails up; and requires us to do the sweaty, muscle-bound work with whatever muse we choose. The rigor is the part of creativity that is often missed—or avoided. But it is essential if we are ever to go about the work of creativity in a sustained way.

Ben Batory is a senior vice president of trading at Franklin Templeton Investments. He explained to me how he learned to normalize rigor while working on the trading floor.

> Sitting on a trading desk and attempting to solve an incredibly complicated daily puzzle always inspires wonder and wide eyes: news crosses the ticker tape, people react, stocks move, fortunes are made or lost, lives are affected. It's incredible to witness firsthand.
>
> Every day requires rigor, but early on was the toughest. I learned from the equivalent of drill sergeants who barked things like "We don't make mistakes, EVER" and "We stay up all night and never miss the market open the next day" and "We get every trade right" and "We don't get sick, we don't complain." Every day just requires an intense focus. But then, like anything, it becomes normal.
>
> As it turns out, wonder requires an active, rigorous, steady, disciplined approach to sustain it. In short, wonder requires rigor! Granted, that sounds counterintuitive, right? You'd think wonder and rigor would be antonyms.

Ben's last comment reflects that he also understands the intersection of wonder and rigor. Rigor ensures that we actually complete the leap we started. It sustains the necessary momentum to create something tangible. Rigor is the grit and resilience that creativity requires for the long haul. It is the accumulation of commitment and knowledge needed to follow through, to get to value, to get to innovation.

THE WONDER RIGOR PARADIGM

Did you know it is possible to touch the invisible? That is what perfumers do. As perfumer at IFF, International Flavors and Fragrances, in New York, Celine Barel produces the haute couture of scent. She plays at creating "olfactive vision." On a visit to IFF, I observed synesthetic phrases being thrown around among Celine and her colleagues as they described perfume variations that were in development: *This smells very wet. I like the gourmand. This one is like a sticky sweet candy.*

When Celine was in business school, her banking friends admired the ways she was applying a business degree to what seemed for them the intangible nature of perfume. She knew that she was actually developing a superpower: the ability to create the presence of someone who is absent. Perfume was her avenue for doing so. And like me, she uses a hybrid approach to tap into her creativity and develop new, innovative products.

For Celine, wonder and rigor are at the heart of scent creation. It starts with vision, dreaming, and exploring. But it also requires rigorous experimentation and keeping track of exact chemical formulas. Celine must work through tons of ambiguity because there are so many unknowns in the journey of perfume creation. A lot can change, from the fields of flowers to the compounding of the fragrance in the labs to when the scent finally lands on a person's skin and is inhaled. Despite that uncertainty, she must remain confident that through her disciplined work her olfactive vision will be realized.

As Celine's story shows, the wonder rigor paradigm consists of two important principles.

1. Rigor cannot be sustained without wonder.

Many companies across the United States have declared that they are innovative, yet they have neglected to make the time to design processes, systems, and spaces that allow for creativity. This is because they start at the wrong place. They fall in love with the business-value results of innovation instead of with the processes that will make their employees innovative. Consequently, they get caught up in procedure, rulebooks, and meetings—all elements of rigor that are necessary but, without also allowing for wonder, lead to churn and fatigue in the organization. What is needed are intentionally designed moments and spaces for wonder: the permission to ask audacious questions; experiences at work that allow for awe; and opportunities to physically and metaphorically wander and get lost in ideas.

2. Wonder is found in the midst of rigor.
The corollary to the above is that wonder can be generated from the tedium of rigor. Think back to a routine task you have set for yourself: weeding the garden, cleaning the woodwork on stair banisters, threading a needle, doing your taxes, solving a difficult math problem, or preparing the agenda for a meeting. It is often in the midst of rote labor that wonder emerges. A new idea sparks within you, or you suddenly see things from a slightly different perspective. This is because rigor requires intense and deep ways to see, observe, and listen—the same practices required for creativity.

Paul Zak is a neuroeconomist, researcher, professor, and entrepreneur. He is probably most well known for his 2011 TED Talk, when he introduced himself to the world as "Dr. Love" and shared his research on the hormone oxytocin and trust. I met him at a conference where I was speaking, and where his company Immersion Neuroscience was measuring the emotional responses that the audience was having to the presentations throughout the day. Wonder comes into play quite a bit in the midst of Paul's rigorous research. He explained to me:

> We don't value one finding over another in my world. There's lots of noise. So it's this wonder—or skepticism— that pushes us to look at data, run experiments again.

After years of this, you gain a profound understanding. But you don't get to have the wonder without the rigor!

Jim Caruso is an accountant's accountant. He's the chief financial officer at Simplura Health Group. He loves the precision of numbers and the way a balance sheet tells a story:

> My work is all about rigor. Accounting is about rules and proscribed forms. The due diligence for M&A's is hugely rigorous. There are lots of issue lists, question lists, and interview lists. I consider myself a process person, and I love process itself. I guess I am always trying to make order out of chaos.

Fortunately for me, Jim was not so numbers bound that he was unwilling to explore the wonder rigor paradigm. He became a faculty member in the Strategic Design MBA program I developed. In his accounting career there have been many times when he has had to pull teams out of the minutiae and help them see the bigger picture. His ability to help others zoom out, set aside the checklist, and redesign the process comes from his hobbies. For one, Jim enjoys reading about behavioral economics, the human reasons behind how we make economic decisions. He's also a practitioner of the martial art Brazilian jiu-jitsu, which he describes as human chess. Third, Jim is a tornado chaser. It illuminates why he was willing to experiment with integrating the iterative design thinking process into an accounting course. Jim says he was always fascinated by storms as a kid. At the beginning, he would go on tours with storm-chasing companies. Now, Jim doesn't need a tour guide when chasing tornadoes. When I asked him why he chases storms, the wonder and rigor paradigm came alive:

> Tornadoes have a sense of energy, power, and connectedness. There's a physical exhilaration, pattern recognition, and intuition involved. And there's also an analytical

side to it. There are things I understand as rules of thumb without completely understanding the physics.

Chasing tornadoes allows Jim to physically engage in both wonder—the awesomeness of the experience—and rigor—nature's calculated perfection that allows so many variables to conspire into one storm.

The process of asking big, expansive questions and pushing the limits of a situation in audacious ways is full of wonder. It is unhinged from the constraints of "We've always done it this way" or "We tried that 15 years ago and it didn't work!" Wondrous questions lead to divergent thinking. Meanwhile, rigorous questions, the ones that typically start with "How might we . . . ?" lead to convergent thinking. Toggling between the two is how you build a creative competency. As you practice inquiry, improvisation, and intuition to solve problems, you will necessarily and effortlessly shift between wonder and rigor.

Riding a bike, baking a cake, learning how to dance: these are all examples of activities where we are constantly working at the intersection of wonder and rigor. The engineering of the bicycle itself is an example of rigor, where the exact placement of wheel and spokes makes all the difference in the world. Additionally, we can all recall the intense amount of concentration and effort it took to learn how to ride a bicycle. In addition to my dance classes, it was the most rigor I had ever applied to anything in my life up to the ripe age of seven. The frustration, necessary repetition, and redundant failure of falling off the bike over and over again were tedious—and frankly, not fun. But my, the leap into finally getting it right, flying down the sidewalk on my banana seat without training wheels for the first time, and experiencing my block in completely new ways—that was the wonder.

In a TEDx Talk, Christine Cox, cofounder of the Philadelphia premiere contemporary ballet company BalletX, referenced both the athleticism (rigor) and the artistry (wonder) required to tell stories through dance. Dancers are systems designers. Similar to designers and engineers, they also are kinesthetic learners who must move and make, prod and rework in order to discover, zoom in and out, and gain new perspective. They integrate both discipline and audacious dreaming to do their best work. It is not enough for a dancer (or any artist) to be technically proficient and rigorous in their approach. In order to move us, they must bring an additional element to their work: wonder.

WONDER AND RIGOR MAKE CREATIVITY ACCESSIBLE

I used to be shy about introducing my WonderRigor™ model to my corporate clients. I worried that they would find it a bit "woo-woo" and too loosey-goosey. But the opposite was true. When I would tentatively introduce the WonderRigor framework, usually at the end of a meeting, after all of the "important stuff" had been discussed, their eyes would light up. They sat up a bit straighter and began asking me lots of questions about ways they might apply the model to their own teams. It turns out that understanding creativity from this perspective has an engaging and democratizing effect.

People are trying to figure out how to do innovation work in a sustained way so that it can become part of the overall culture. When I share this perspective of toggling between wonder and rigor and using tactics that we can all access—inquiry, improvisation, and intuition—it opens up new possibilities. As one client group at VaynerMedia shared with me, "We need to make room for creative wonder despite the fast pace and rigor. Our work will become higher quality and more efficient if we collaborate more across disciplines with things like workshops and jam sessions on a consistent basis."

Next we will explore that first tactic of inquiry and how both wonder and rigor lead to asking better questions.

 CREATIVITY LEAP EXERCISE

FOR YOU

► Try floating. Floating centers are popping up in cities around the world. In a 90-minute floating session you immerse yourself in a tank full of very warm water and about 800 pounds of sea salt—approximating the environment of the Dead Sea—so that you float. It is completely dark and silent around you. You emerge more relaxed and attuned to your environment. It feels like an emotional tune-up. Sensory deprivation does wonders for sparking wondrous thinking.

► Commit to repetition. For example, identify the counterpoint to your hobby that requires deep focus and redundancy to get it right. For me, it is methodically stretching my body. I take at least one stretch class per week, and spend about 15 minutes a couple of days a week stretching. It makes the dance class part a lot easier!

FOR YOUR ORGANIZATION

► Build in mini-celebrations. Don't wait for the holiday party or the summer barbecue to give recognition. This type of incentive goes miles in building up wonder.

► Set aside one hour a week for a Rigor Sprint, a deep-dive focus on a particular question. The question could be around a client's problem or related to an internal bottleneck at the office that needs a workaround. Allow people to go off to their own sequestered areas to work quietly and then report back.

CHAPTER 3

INQUIRE
ASK A BETTER FRIGGIN' QUESTION

WHY WE DON'T ASK BETTER QUESTIONS

The lack of an appetite for building inquiry starts with our educational systems. I learned this firsthand as I attended four very different types of schools between kindergarten and 12th grade. I transitioned from a crunchy-granola preschool to an urban public elementary school in Philadelphia with a more rote-learning environment. There I was great at completing worksheets and collecting lots of gold star stickers. However, the lack of evidence that the school was cultivating my intellectual capacity and promise was extremely frustrating to my parents. Thus in the fourth grade they switched me to a suburban public school where the education was more rigorous and I learned the fundamentals of reading, writing, and arithmetic. But the social environment was challenging for me, as I was the only black child in my grade. My younger sister and I literally doubled the ethnic minority representation in the entire school overnight.

I then went to a private Quaker prep school from 7th through 12th grades where the culture of learning was entirely new for me. My peers and I were rewarded for challenging our teachers, asking better questions than our classmates, and craftily begging forgiveness—not permission. While this elite learning environment was hard for me to adapt to initially, I quickly caught on. I experienced a kind of liberation by learning how to frame better questions. Inquiry allowed me to explore my preexisting norms and other terrain in new ways.

There's a physiological reason why it's hard to build a culture of inquiry. Feedback is challenging because it threatens our identity and connection to the larger group. Most of us don't experience feedback and critical questions as a positive experience. In *Feedback (and Other Dirty Words): Why We Fear It, How to Fix It*, author M. Tamra Chandler talks about the "fight, flight, or freeze" reaction when our amygdala, at the base of the brain, is triggered.[1] The limbic system is considered the "primitive brain," while the prefrontal cortex is considered the "wise brain." When we get feedback, our limbic system codes it as a threat. Once the amygdala is activated, critique triggers the sympathetic nervous system and stress hormones. Neurotransmitters get released, and we have a physical reaction. We start to focus on survival and either lash out or shut down. In short, we lose perspective. We feel as if our identity is literally being challenged, and on a primal level we fear being banished from the tribe and deserted. Who wouldn't react with a racing heart, sweaty palms, dilated pupils, and shortened breath?

In other cases, those who ask the big questions are ignored or even penalized. In 2019, Boeing experienced a series of tragic crashes with its 737 Max planes. These 737s entered the commercial market in 2017 and were equipped with an MCAS system, which stabilizes the plane by pushing the nose down. The problem was that many pilots were not thoroughly trained on the system, nor was the MCAS system included in some manuals. Questions started there, but they weren't thoroughly vetted.

Of additional concern was a second report from the *New York Times* about the number of factory workers who expressed quality control concerns about the Boeing Dreamliner, a different Boeing aircraft, with production in a South Carolina plant. Workers found debris dangerously close to the plane's engine. When questions and concerns were raised, they were dismissed largely due to time-to-market speed needs to make the production quota. One factory worker, John "Swampy" Barnett, who continued to question the shoddy work, ultimately filed a whistleblower claim and left Boeing. He asserted, "I haven't seen a plane out of Charleston yet that I'd put my name on saying it's safe and airworthy."[2]

While it has become popular in organizations to say that questions are embraced, employees often feel differently. They equate asking questions mostly with ignorance, not with inquiry. They are not convinced that they should risk humiliation or, worse yet, being fired for upsetting the status quo. But you can't generate something new and novel with the status quo.

A culture of inquiry is hindered by several things. First, we've got web search engines in close proximity in our handbags and jeans pockets. The convenience of search algorithms has rendered us lazy and less willing to explore in depth—unless that depth consists of plunging down the rabbit hole of YouTube "If you liked this"-style prompts.

Second, we are pressed for time. Our days are compounded by deadlines. We reward speed much more than we reward depth. In actuality, the best scenario is to work, think, and act with both breadth and depth. This multipronged approach gets better as you become more skilled in asking questions.

Last, and perhaps most important, a culture of inquiry requires more of that sitting with ambiguity we discussed in earlier chapters. This is difficult, because our society is biased toward the rational. We are infatuated with big data that is quantitative in nature. We feel more comfortable in a hard-and-fast-solutions orientation, full of Gantt charts, agendas, and plans. The messy, open-ended nature of inquiry is disorienting, and asking better questions obligates us to move away from an obsession with finding a single, clear solution toward falling in love with problems and the process.

INQUIRY IS THE MESSY PROCESS OF MOVING FROM WHY TO HOW

Nicole Pittman knows quite a bit about falling in love with problems. Nicole is an attorney, founder of the Center on Youth Registration Reform and one of our country's leading child advocates and policy experts on child sex offenders. She started her career as a public defender and witnessed firsthand that many laws weren't helpful to children. That led her down the path of national policy reform. She observed to me, "Our system actually traumatizes trauma. We are looking for healing but actually committing more violence (via the system) to the most vulnerable: children." That realization drove Nicole to be guided by the following question: "Why do we criminalize childhood?" Nicole continually integrates wonder and rigor to effect systems change. She told me the following story about her process in child advocacy work:

> So much of my discovery came from doing interviews on the road around the country with these kids—so the narrative shifted for me. I really wanted to see who these "bad kids" were—and I couldn't find any. . . . I realized I would need new people to engage: Republicans and Democrats, law enforcement and survivors. I forged new alliances. . . . I continually reminded myself

that "this is a child." The kids who were on registry helped me connect the dots.

All of the rigorous inquiry that Nicole has done prepared her to shift her work upstream. Today she is developing the Roadmap Initiative, which will adopt a systems design approach to change the way we think about children. She has been inspired by the Dagara tribe of West Africa, whose philosophy is that at conception parents create a song that becomes the child's identity. That song is most important for *when* (not if) the child strays. The lesson is that being reminded of your identity is the best cure for straying away. Nicole's creativity has helped her to do this work by constantly starting with wonder and new questions in spite of how complex a problem child sex offense is.

We think that by playing it safe and not asking questions, we stay docked in the safe harbor of certainty. In fact, we end up getting stranded in the shallow waters of "We've always done it this way." If we don't get good at framing new and different questions to understand why a competitor, or someone younger than us, or someone from a completely different culture does things a certain way, then we are working at a disadvantage.

Knowing how to ask and frame questions is a discipline. You have to be thoughtful and intentional about how you frame a question in order to obtain the most insight from a person. Heidi Zak, cofounder of the online bra company ThirdLove, shared with me the ways she likes to phrase questions to her team. She wants to ensure that she provokes their creative thinking, instead of shutting down conversation in an intimidating way.

> Our values on the wall are all about challenging the status quo. This company was built on defying conventions. . . . If I'm not asking questions, then I am in my own world and I'm not connecting. I ask lots of questions when people present. I think that "why" questions

can sometimes be too pointed. "How" and "what" are better. Like, "How did you come to that conclusion?" instead of asking them, "Why did you come to that conclusion?" I allow a person to describe their thought process in a positive way for information gathering.

In some ways, learning how to be a better question-asker is the easy part. The more challenging part is figuring out how to normalize inquiry in an organization so that it becomes part of the culture. Warren Berger, author of *A More Beautiful Question*, investigated the effectiveness of inquiry-driven leadership when he identified that the companies we think of as innovative, like Google, Apple, and Zappos, are actually quite good at leading with questions. He found that they start with asking "Why?" and then "What if?" and then land on "How?" sorts of questions. They start with divergent, big-picture, wonder-driven thinking and move to convergent, rigorous, and applied thinking.

An inquiry-led company may start by asking, "Why aren't we selling any products in the Southern Hemisphere?" or "Why do we recruit only from Ivy League universities?" It would then transition to some good "What if?" questions, such as "What if we started selling our products in Brazil?" or "What if we started recruiting from community colleges and sought out older adults with impressive work experience but a not-so-pedigreed formal education?" Finally, they might land on tactical "How?" questions, such as, "How can we start establishing contacts in Brazil?" and "How will we build relationships with less traditional educational institutions?"

Each phase of inquiry requires wonder—for discovery—and rigor—to ensure standards. It begins with leaders who model that exploring, prodding, and poking at the status quo is OK—like the heads of REC (Resources for Every Creator) Philly and Vectorworks.

REC Philly is a coworking network and platform to help artists make their passions profitable. It was founded on the principle that proximity builds collaboration. Its cofounders, Will Toms and Dave Silver, started out focusing on event production and decided to pivot away from their production company after asking the question, "How can artists access the resources they need in one place?"

The question sparked their curiosity, and through their tacit (not tangible) experience, they gained the confidence to make a creativity leap into a new venture. They ended up launching REC Philly in an old window factory in North Philly that had other studio tenants.

"We posed lots of questions. Sometimes your gut is smarter than your mind. That helped us shift to a focus on mission," said Will. (We will explore how those gut feelings fuel creativity much more deeply in chapter 5.)

Biplab Sarkar, the CEO of software firm Vectorworks, shared with me a time when, during one of their Innovation Weeks, his team asked, "Why can't we use iPhones like a TV remote?" They then worked on how to control one of their computer applications via a smartphone, and it eventually became an offering to clients. Vectorworks ensures that questions can emerge from all corners and layers of the company by instilling an idea log. Everyone knows that not all ideas will be implemented, but at least all ideas will be vetted. They now have a database, internally sourced, for new ideas, questions, and solutions that can be revisited at any time. Biplab acknowledged, however, that building a culture of inquiry has not happened overnight:

> It took us about five years. It was a lot of struggle because there were departments who weren't talking to each other. So we had to make lots of changes to get to where we are today. Now people have mentors, and managers have information sources. This makes people curious.

TRUST IS THE FOUNDATION OF INQUIRY

I'm from Philadelphia, and our NBA team, the 76ers, has made "Trust the process" synonymous with their brand. To admit that you do not know something requires humility, self-awareness, and—in these times—courage. The fundamental building block for that courage is trust. When you put yourself out there to reveal that you have a question or an uncertainty, or you are just allowing your mind to wander and explore an idea from another angle, the environment must be primed for trust. Each time you raise your hand, you are trusting that a big emotional safety net will be in place. Leading with questions is one of the ways an organization can prime an environment with trust, so that employees feel the courage to share not only what is on their mind, but also what's in their imagination.

When we ask a question, we might reveal our own ignorance. That ignorance might then be penalized with critique. And that critique could result in our losing a sense of identity and connection to our group. This is a primal fear. Consider that we all know instinctively, as young as nursery school age, that the cruelest form of punishment we can inflict is to isolate and ignore another person. We carry that fear of disconnection and isolation through our adulthood.

Safiya Noble, an associate professor at the University of California, Los Angeles, and author of *Algorithms of Oppression: How Search Engines Reinforce Racism*, shared with me this story about the value of trust from early in her career. On a Sunday morning, her mother died. Safiya was scheduled to lead a call the very next day. When Safiya called her boss to share the tragic news, the boss's response was cold and unsympathetic.

> I was lying on my back in my mom's bed, enveloped in grief, and I remember my boss saying, "You wrote this marketing plan, and we need you on the call." I felt a

disconnect between my work and my humanness as a daughter.

That moment shifted my relationship to my work. What I learned in that moment was that I actually couldn't be creative in the face of my humanity being completely erased. There was no space available by my coworkers for my humanness.

Safiya also had to brave the fear of alienation when she incorporated her humanness into her academic research. Typically, academic scholarship is considered more rigorous if it is deemed objective. Any reference to self is considered too subjective. Yet, it was when Safiya turned inward and began to formulate questions based on her own identity and experiences that she distinguished herself as a thought leader and inclusive technology expert.

I was one of the first scholars to use black feminism to examine the internet. Technology is not neutral. I had to trust my own self-reflection as valid. I used my own experience as the epicenter of where good ideas come from. . . . I realized that I had insights and a lens that was valuable. I'm grateful that I trusted myself.

Safiya trusted the questions that originated from her own self-reflection and cultural experience. This was a courageous act in light of the norms of objectivity that her doctoral advisory team expected. What if organizations could, like Safiya, flip the negative paradigm on asking questions and critique by building positive cultures?

Trusting that you are valued for who you are as a person is essential to a culture of inquiry. We need connection and acknowledgment of our basic human worth. When this does not happen at regular intervals, it dampens people's ability to give of their creative selves, to ask the big questions that move us forward. As Safiya put it, "There needs to be deposits into the universal bank of goodwill because sometimes we will have to draw down."

Trust is where Dag Folger and Peter Knutson begin when working with clients. Dag is a cofounder of A+I (Architecture Plus Information), and Peter is a principal and director of strategy. Their firm designs spaces and strategy. When we spoke about their work process, they started with the principle of trust.

> Part of the creative process is about opening futures up and closing futures off. The last thing to ask a client is "What kind of office space do you want?" Instead, we ask them "How do you feel at work? Who do you like to talk to? When are you most motivated? Most productive?" . . . Spending the time to build the responsible sense of trust—to interpret and reinterpret what they are trying to achieve—is key.

One of the outcomes A+I has experienced from building in discovery time and inquiry is that they come across unusual characters who are primary in the design process:

> A lot of the creative decisions are happening in the accounting department. The accountants are actually designing the project in advance of it being handed to the architects. When they build a spreadsheet, it's identifying how to schedule and staff a project. There is a lot of design in the sequencing of the staff and schedule. Designing a spreadsheet is actually a part of the creative process.

Their inquiry period broadens and democratizes the reality of who is creative.

Bridgewater Associates is a different example of how the principle of trust can manifest within an organization.

Bridgewater is an American hedge fund with over $130 billion of assets under management. At their offices, all conversations in the company are recorded. Yes, that's right, recorded. There's nowhere to hide or office door to close so that you can tell your colleague what you *really* think but couldn't say during the meeting. Ray Dalio, Bridgewater's founder and president, would rather everything be openly recorded so that there is complete transparency. He believes that such transparency gets people closer to truth telling and truth asking.

Dalio's goal is to build an organizational culture where there is "meaningful work and meaningful relationship through radical truth and radical transparency." He insists that this radical transparency is the difference between a mediocre company full of office politics and a highly efficient company that runs like a well-oiled machine. He wants to be surrounded by people who openly disagree with him because it helps him see his blind spots.

Such a culture is not for everyone. Approximately 30 percent of new Bridgewater hires do not last beyond their first 18 months on the job. But Dalio thinks this is a good thing. An aggressive attrition moves the company closer to an authentic culture where people are saying what they really mean to each other. No matter how creepy some of us may find such an atmosphere, there is something to be said for an environment that avoids behind-the-back shaming in order to build the trust that is essential for deep inquiry.

In an interview with *New York Times* reporter Andrew Ross Sorkin at the *Times'* DealBook conference in 2014, Dalio asked, "Wouldn't you rather know what people are really thinking, or not? Isn't it weird that in most of our organizations we don't know?"[3] This perspective—that having transparent insight into how others think and the questions they raise makes you more effective—is a provocative one. His goal in all of this is "to determine what is true." His big question: "Why can't we civilly and thoughtfully disagree?" Dalio insists that it is unethical not to have critical and thoughtful discussions where we question each other and respectfully disagree with one another.

As I listened to the interview, I felt myself having an emotional and physical reaction. Emotionally, I experienced a bit of nervousness as I imagined myself in such a work environment. It felt a bit Orwellian upon first hearing it. Physically, I felt my shoulders stiffen and start to hunch over.

My reaction to a scenario where I would be exposed to constant questioning and radical transparency is not inconsequential. It is linked to the way our brain is designed. My prefrontal cortex, or "wise brain," was saying, "Yes, of course I would like clarity to understand what others are thinking." Meanwhile, my limbic, reptilian brain, where my fight-or-flight response lives, was going into defense mode: "Will I be harmed? Will the tribe reject me if they don't like what I'm saying? If I ask this question, will I be thrown out?"

So we have this tug of war between wanting to know, wanting the transparency, and then defending ourselves from being opened up to rejection. But, as Dalio reminds us, these responses are just habits, and we can form new habits to be receptive to the questions, exposure, and transparency. At Bridgewater, they estimate that it takes a year and a half for new employees to become accustomed to the Bridgewater culture of radical transparency, to form the new habits that welcome being recorded as a means to greater respect and effectiveness.

The recorded conversations that Bridgewater inventories have had some practical results. One is that there is no spin—not on information, and not on people. Second, you have data about your own behavior, which means there is more clarity around what you do well and poorly. For example, Dalio has realized that he is not good at the details and is very forgetful. Third, because people are incentivized to be honest about the good and the bad, there is less room for dubious and nefarious

dealings. As a result, Dalio said, in the 40 years that Bridgewater has been in existence, they have had only three frivolous
lawsuits.[4]

Bridgewater is a living, breathing prototype of the kind of
organization that Jeremy Heimans and Henry Timms wrote
about in *New Power: How Power Works in Our Hypercon-
nected World—and How to Make It Work for You*. According
to the authors, organizations that wield "old power" values
are full of bureaucracy, discretion, specialization, and a separation between the private and public spheres. Alternatively,
companies like Bridgewater that exhibit "new power" values
are characterized by informality, open-source collaboration,
self-organization, and radical transparency. You have to admit,
radical transparency is a novel way to deal with the ambiguity
of not knowing.

NORMALIZING INQUIRY WITHIN YOUR ORGANIZATION

How a company sustains an inquiry-based culture is a nuanced
thing. It starts with leadership, yes—but it also requires
everyone to think about where opportunities are for fostering
curiosity. In his book *Curious: The Desire to Know and Why
Your Future Depends on It*, Ian Leslie explains that curiosity
is the result of an information gap. To be curious about something, you must know just a little bit about it. He writes, "In
order to feel curious—to feel the desire to close an information
gap—you have to be aware of a gap in your own knowledge in
the first place."[5] What better way is there to become aware of
information gaps and drive that consciousness than by setting
up environments where there is diversity of thought, ethnicity,
age, gender, and class?

The educational nonprofit Leadership+Design (L+D) tries to
vet for creativity and difference during the interview process.
For example, they ask candidates to include a photograph of an

artifact that tells L+D who they are as a person and to explain why they selected the artifact. When we are surrounded by people who are different from us, it's like walking around with a gigantic magnifying glass projected onto ourselves. Our own assumptions, peculiarities, and biases get accentuated. This is a good thing. It is only through the discovery of what we don't know that we are prompted to go off course to ask different, better questions.

Most of us find psychological safety in being around people who think like us. Otherwise, friction results. We assume that it is best to avoid the friction and that the process will go a lot more smoothly if we work with people who by and large think the way we do. Well, the process might go more smoothly, but the outcome will not necessarily be better.

When Jerry Hirshberg was the president of Nissan Design International, he flipped the paradigm on friction. He emphasized the need for diverse teams that could approach problems from a range of perspectives. He insisted that colleagues from sales, marketing, manufacturing, and finance join his designers in the problem-solving process. He understood that the outcome of friction is energy. So why not convert the energy from friction into something positive? He called the messiness that resulted "creative abrasion."

When we form teams of people with different skill sets, that thought diversity naturally leads us to ask more interesting questions. I could never think to ask the sorts of questions you would and vice versa. That is a really important acknowledgment. The more diverse the inputs, the more innovative the output.

We can also design triggers, routines, and rewards to shift behavior to normalizing inquiry, the way Tamera Maresh-Carver at FedEx Express did. Tamera is the managing director of global learning and development at FedEx Express in Memphis, Tennessee. Her trigger is to keep asking, "Why not?" and

"What if?" when presented with a problem—like the one she found in 2018.

Tamera realized that only 2.6 percent of FedEx Express employees took advantage of the company's tuition reimbursement program. By asking "Why not?" she uncovered all sorts of barriers to entry that she and her team could remove one by one, such as the financial strain of paying the initial fees out of pocket prior to reimbursement and the fact that a low grade on a required course would make tuition reimbursement negligible.

> I would hear comments like "I want them to have skin in the game," but people already do when they put themselves in that position.

Yet another barrier was access: partnering universities had to make their courses available online.

> These folks work at night, and they may share a car with a person at home. They could be taking care of their own kids and an adult parent, so whatever we developed with a university had to be self-paced.

The last big barrier was the standardized tests that most universities require applicants to take. It was not a realistic expectation for a 42-year-old high school graduate, for example, with years of work experience, who had not looked at a test in decades.

> We didn't want them to have to take a standardized test to prove that they were college material. This is a systemic barrier to become part of the academic world. So we came up with another way to prove their commitment and that they had moxie. [Our partner] the University of Memphis came up with the Prep Academy program. It's equivalent to 12 credits and is

a mastery-based program with no grades. They keep working until they pass the course.

As of this writing, one year since the inception of the Prep Academy program, 15 percent of FedEx Express employees have taken advantage of the tuition reimbursement program, a 12-point increase. By framing new questions, FedEx Express and the University of Memphis made a creativity leap that is changing FedEx Express employees' lives.

INQUIRY SPARKS DISCOVERY

Inquiry requires us to observe and listen more actively in order to frame better questions. The process of moving from why to what-if to how ensures that we remain engaged with our work, colleagues, and clients. For our organizations it is insurance that we don't fall into the trap of a superiority complex and a too-big-to-fail attitude. It ensures that we never settle for the status quo.

But inquiry is often just the first step. Discovery comes from adding in the rigor of prodding and investigating further to determine what lies ahead and what might have been missed. We need to get comfortable with what results from leaping into newly discovered territory. We must learn how to work without a script, with minimal structures. That is the essence of improvisation, and it is what we will explore next, in chapter 4.

CREATIVITY LEAP EXERCISE

FOR YOU
► Interview a colleague. Spend time devising at least 20 questions, and then prioritize five of those questions. What new things did you learn about the colleague's life? About his or her professional journey? What lessons can you incorporate back into your own life?

FOR YOUR ORGANIZATION
► Crowdsource questions from your employees and create a catalog of questions about work processes, your industry, and your competitors. This could be done as simply as setting aside wall space with butcher paper and marker pens nearby. It could be as sophisticated as a digital archive. Remember that asking questions is a way of thinking. You can make it anonymous or aim for radical transparency as at Bridgewater.

CHAPTER 4

IMPROVISE
LEVERAGE ORGANIZED CHAOS

THE FUTURE OF WORK IS JAZZ

My relationship to jazz permeates deeply in my life. It was part of the soundscape of my childhood because my dad was a passionate jazz devotee. He learned how to play the acoustic upright bass while serving in the US Air Force in the early 1960s, straight out of high school. His collection of Blue Note jazz albums was well worn. He studied the liner notes. He was the sort of person who could recall within the first eight measures of an Art Blakey recording who was playing trumpet and who was on piano. I marveled at that.

I didn't get jazz immediately. At first, it was just a way for me to cozy up to my dad and spend time with him. He loved taking my sister and me to outdoor summer concerts that went on way past our bedtime. It wasn't until years later that the music disseminated beyond my ears and into my heart. It became an emotional connection to my father and a personal connection to my African-American culture.

In 1960, the iconic jazz vocalist Ella Fitzgerald and her quartet (pianist Paul Smith, guitarist Jim Hall, bassist Wilfred Middlebrooks, drummer Gus Johnson) toured Europe to great acclaim. In a live performance at the Deutschlandhalle arena in Berlin, Germany, she began singing "Mack the Knife." It was a song she'd sung before, but around the second stanza, she suddenly drew a blank. Did the great songstress freeze? Nope. She improvised—and in a self-effacing, cheerful way. You can hear her laughing at herself as she plows through making up words and scatting her way through the rest of the song, with her quartet fully supporting her all along the way. That recording went on to win a Grammy Award in 1961 for Best Female Pop Vocal performance. In 1999 it was inducted into the Grammy Hall of Fame.

The jazz saxophone player Charlie Parker said, "You've got to learn your instrument. Then you practice, practice, practice. And then, when you finally get up there on the bandstand, forget all that and just wail." That, to me, is the essence of improvisation—and the essence of jazz.

Jazz is the preeminent example of a complex system: adaptive, self-organizing, and emergent. The future of work in our increasingly complex world requires us to adopt the chaordic, improvisational methods of jazz musicians.

Coined by Dee Hock, founding CEO of VISA, the credit card company, *chaord* is used to describe the chaos and order that are both present in complex systems. That's right, the VISA card that is in your wallet is part of a history that embraced organized chaos. When Hock was tasked with building VISA, a global platform for the virtual exchange of currency, he quickly realized that trying to build such a complex system at scale would require a departure from the typical organizational chart. He observed that nature abounds with systems that thrive in the midst of some chaos and some order. Keep in mind that chaos

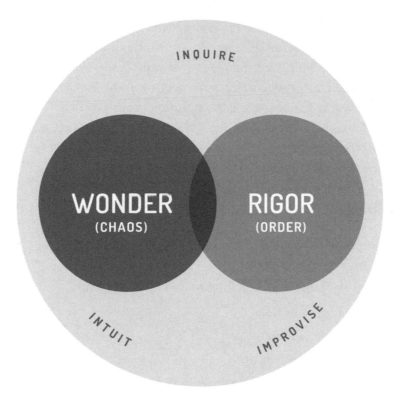

**Figure 3. Toggle between wonder and rigor
(a chaordic system) to solve problems.**

is not anarchy; it is randomness. And order is not control; it is structure. Wonder and rigor are parallel manifestations of the chaos and order in a chaordic system (see Figure 3).

Jazz music thrives on both the chaos and the order emblematic of chaordic systems. The jazz musician must know music theory; master chord progression; and be able to compose songs with at least the minimal structure of a beginning, a middle, and an end. This is the order component. The chaos is the magic that happens in the interstices. It is the random interplay between musicians responding to one another in the moment, self-organizing themselves, and adapting to shifts and changes in key and tempo. Often the leader is embedded so deep inside the quartet or sextet that you cannot tell who is leading and who is following. Or even more to the point, different musicians take turns supporting and emerging as the leader. What if we worked more like this in our human organizations?

Frank Barrett, an academic and jazz musician himself, has written at length in *Yes to the Mess: Surprising Leadership Lessons from Jazz* about what organizations can learn from jazz.[1] Most helpful are his seven principles, which can be summarized in the following characteristics of jazz musicians:

1. Provoke competence

2. Embrace mistakes

3. Use minimal structures to maximize flexibility

4. Distribute tasks

5. Borrow from the past

6. Value hanging out

7. Switch back and forth between following and leading

If you can add even two of those principles to your daily work, imagine what a game changer that would be. For example, what would meetings look like if every now and then junior-level colleagues or people new to the company were invited to lead a meeting? Or if your workplace were designed to allow for more casual hanging out? Or if your manager used mistakes as a launching pad for new discoveries?

I don't get to work from a script every day. None of us do. If you had to visualize your typical day, chances are it would not resemble a linear series of boxes and arrows. More likely it would look like a bunch of squiggly doodle lines that went off in different directions and converged here and there. And then you would start all over again the next day. Life's ambiguity is not diminishing.

DESIGNING IMPROVISATIONAL ORGANIZATIONS

The increased pace of life and faster rates of change require two things of us: first, to build in more pauses and rest to process the flurry of change; second, to reorient ourselves to improvising—this is how we not only navigate but also leverage the ambiguity. It is how we fill the vacuum that wonder opens up with its pregnant pauses at the edge of discovery.

Dee Hock's book *One from Many: VISA and the Rise of Chaordic Organization* is part memoir and part explanation of chaordic systems.[2] In it, Hock details his rationale and process for designing VISA as a chaordic organization in its early stages. There now exists an entire body of scholarship called *chaordic systems thinking*, or CST. These academics, spearheaded by Frans M. van Eijnatten and other CST practitioners, occasionally convene and publish papers on how CST can help companies become learning organizations and transform. CST is one method to navigate complexity.

What we have learned from CST is that clear structure in organizations establishes goalposts and guidelines. But with too much structure, you wind up with a permission-slip culture that can suffocate and stifle people. Employees don't feel like they have any agency to make decisions. Rather, organizations need minimal or fluid structures that allow for chaos and random connections. When both chaos and order are present, an essential fluidity occurs—as at the Ritz-Carlton.

In a global company like the Ritz-Carlton, it is essential that process and procedure are designed to allow for adaptive behavior. Take, for example, the improvisational structure of their lineup meetings. At these meetings, held daily by every department at every property around the world, teams review what to expect for the shift. This short meeting structure conditions employees to be reflective and to listen and learn from one another. In those meetings, they also share and dissect the chaos that is part and parcel of their work in the form of "MR. BIVs"— that is, mistakes, revisions, breakdowns, inefficiencies, and variations. By openly stating and owning whatever is going wrong, employees exercise their capacity to adapt, learn, and grow. This obviously is not something that comes easily. We all shy away from owning what hasn't gone well. But this ritual of wonder and rigor helps them bring order to the chaos of their daily work.

Collaboration doesn't come from a bunch of meetings. True collaboration and creative synergy comes through our ability to improvise with one another. A great example of this is in the restaurant business. Melissa Koujakian is the director of operations at the popular République restaurant in Los Angeles. She uses wonder and rigor to manage the organized chaos of dinner shifts.

First, the ritual that she leads at the pre-shift meeting gives structure to her staff, who will need to anticipate guests' needs and adapt all night. She starts with a loud and enthusiastic salutation: "Welcome to the experience!" It underscores the fact that guests come to dine to have an experience, not just to eat food. The team gets acquainted with the evening's VIP list, and the chef reviews the menu. There is a discussion of any new cocktails and beer, and everyone gets to sample the featured wine. Then the wonder part gets incorporated:

> After all the seriousness, after all the regimented stuff, we play team-building games. For example, if you could be any animal, what would you be and why? If you could live in any country, where and why?
>
> When a *stagiaire* (a new person) is in the circle, they will get asked a ton of bonkers questions like "Would you rather die freezing alive or burning to death?" And then at some point they will be asked, "Why do you want to work with us? What about us makes you want

to be here?" It's validating to the staff. [The games] remind us of our humanity and that our values are pretty universal.

The ritual that the République team engages in nightly to prepare them to improvise has three major lessons we can apply to improving the way we work. Those are being hyperpresent, valuing the outlier, and designing fluid structures.

1. *Being hyperpresent.* One of the basic rules in improvisation is "Yes, and . . . " It is about agreement and building on a concept. It prevents the breakdown of momentum that comes from a "Yes, but . . . " or, even worse, straight-out "No" response. In order to build on the idea that someone has just offered to you, it is required that you engage in deep, intentional listening. It is an exercise in selflessness and generosity to give someone else your rapt attention and then amplify their idea, rather than wait for them to shut up so that you can focus on your own. Imagine if this principle were actively employed in our work environments. Think of the more energizing exchange of ideas we would have. Wonder would increase in value due to the investment we would have in each other's ideas.

2. *Valuing the outlier.* Valuing the perspective of your extreme customer or your most junior staffer can lead to new discoveries, and it also empowers people. It can manifest in organizations as emergent leadership and the improvising of new ways to work according to the client need at hand. In jazz, valuing the outlier manifests as musicians take turns stepping out on solos and then receding to the back to support the next soloist. This is what jazz academic Barrett called "solo and support."

3. *Designing fluid structures.* Ella Fitzgerald's ability to flow in and out of the basic song structure reflects one of the greatest gifts of jazz music. The fact that the music composition was not in a rigid outline meant that she and her fellow musicians could be more adaptive in the moment. This would not necessarily have been the case in the model of a classical orchestra. The ability to work without a script is an essential skill set. But how can you scale improvisation throughout an organization? By ensuring that the rules are embedded in a fluid structure that allows employees to problem-solve in the moment.

LIFE (AND WORK) IS CHAORDIC

John Harker is our family plumber. He's been practicing the craft since age 15, when he began helping his dad in the family business. When I asked him about the ways that creativity shows up in his work, he did not hesitate to say, "Every day I improvise. I see what's behind the wall. All I go in with is my flashlight." He talked in poetic terms about his ability to visualize. John is really a systems designer. His work requires him to coordinate with architects, electricians, and carpenters. He must constantly anticipate their needs.

Oh, that we all had the foresight and nimbleness to improvise in the way that John does. His example demonstrates that the ability to improvise is honed over years and years of practice and experience. Making something new, paradoxically, requires you to be keenly aware of what is past and present. Inventiveness starts with being keenly observant of others around you. Those observations lead to new questions: "Why do they do it that way? How did they figure this out? Who is on their team to help them work in that way? What process do they use?" Inventiveness also requires an awareness of what is lacking right in front of you. Identify the mistakes, the redundancies, and the inadequacies, and then strive to improve them. Generating something new and novel starts with a dissatisfaction with the status quo. A superiority complex and a too-big-to-fail attitude put you at a huge disadvantage. The sense of urgency that upstarts and start-ups have is their elixir. The feeling that competitors are nipping at their heels is their insurance.

The Steelcase "New Work. New Rules" report stated, "The companies that are thriving have learned that teamwork—and the culture that supports it—are the only way to make innovation happen. It turns out that there is an 'I' in team: because teams consist of individuals."[3]

Teams thrive on improvisation. The ability to engage in deep and active listening, the trust to bounce ideas off each other, and the space to iterate and build off of what has come before are all by-products of improvisation. Improvisation requires us to riff with others and sometimes even with ourselves in order to sense our way through a situation. That is one approach for thinking about intuition, I suppose—a type of personal, internal riffing to help you make a decision. Let's dig deeper into the wonder and rigor of intuition in the next chapter.

CREATIVITY LEAP EXERCISE

FOR YOU

► One incremental way to practice improvising is to "quietstorm": this is individualized brainstorming, in silence. Set a timer for 90 seconds, and give yourself a prompt like "What are all the things I could make from a paper coffee cup?" Don't edit yourself, allow for a rapid stream of consciousness—and, better yet, return to the mind-set of your goofy eight-year-old self. Practice quiet-storming on a regular basis. If you're feeling more daring, try taking an improvisation class. Many local theater companies and comedy clubs offer them.

FOR YOUR ORGANIZATION

► Have everyone on your team commit to incorporating into their work project every day at least two of the seven principles that Frank Barrett says we can learn from jazz. Ask them to share how it's going and if they experience any shifts. Then decide as a group if you want to begin to incorporate their new work-around at scale and on a regular basis.

CHAPTER 5

INTUIT
PUT BRAVERY BEFORE MASTERY

THE INS AND OUTS OF INTUITION

At age 19, as a sophomore in college, I was gifted the permission to follow my intuition. I had just called home in tears about a first-world problem: "I don't know what to declare for my major."

My parents had sacrificed a lot for our education, and I didn't want to disappoint them. I wanted to get a "good job" at the end of a really wonderful and very expensive education, but I didn't know what that job should be. My parents asked, "OK . . . what do you mean you don't know what to major in?"

I said, "Well, I almost failed economics, and I think political science is boring, and sociology just reduces people to statistics!" They responded with, "Well, what are you *interested* in?" Apologetically, I began to describe how excited I was by the anthropology and multidisciplinary Africana studies classes I had taken. They listened and then told me, "That's what you should study. Study what you love, and opportunities will come to you." My parents gave me an incredible gift, the permission to do what I loved, and then trust that opportunities would come to me. I have applied that sound advice to follow my heart and my gut at every crossroads of my life since.

What I know now is that going with your intuition is not the luxury that I thought my parents were awarding me. It is actually a primal and strategic tool for survival. That is because intuition gives us an attunement to our surroundings and a real-time distillation of what we should do. It allows us to tune and align when things are subtly off, and to pay attention to emerging signals to make new choices.

Sophy Burnham, author of *The Art of Intuition: Cultivating Your Inner Wisdom*, defines intuition as "a knowing without knowing."[1] Dictionary.com defines intuition as an "ability to understand something immediately, without the need for conscious reasoning." I like to think of intuition as feelings that reside in the mind (brain feelings!), offering up a nice simpatico in the left brain–right brain dynamic.

In this world where we are inundated with data, information, and constant nudging from our phone alerts, how do we tune in to our intuition? After all, intuition requires space and stillness to get to clarity. Intuition is also a form of pattern recognition, and the more we exercise it and pay attention to it, the stronger, clearer, and more flexible it becomes. Conversely, the more we ignore what our intuition is telling us, the dimmer and softer those brain feelings get.

In his 2007 book *Strategic Intuition*, William Duggan highlights three types of intuition: ordinary, expert, and strategic.[2] Ordinary intuition can best be described as a gut feeling—for example, a deep feeling that you should not walk down a particular street or that you should date a particular person. Expert intuition is that which comes from having honed a craft. It allows you to know exactly how to move even without being able to see what's around the corner. The NBA superstar LeBron

James is an example of someone who possesses expert intu- ition. Strategic intuition is slow and clear, and it comes to us in contexts that are very new. It is strategic intuition that becomes the most important in ambiguous work environments.

Western society's trajectory since the first industrial rev- olution has been to prioritize the rational, the material, the machine, and the predictive over the internal realm, the intuitive, and the emotional. But in ambiguous and complex situations with limited (or overwhelming) data and clues, cul- tivating your intuition alongside your intellect is critical. When you can't know or make sense of everything going on around you, integrating heart and mind is the game changer.

As Albert Einstein said, "The intuitive mind is a sacred gift, and the rational mind is a faithful servant. We have created a society that honors the servant and has forgotten the gift."

INTUITION AS A TOOL FOR STRATEGY

Across the board, the leaders I interviewed credited their intuition with their ability to take decisive action. Designer and tech guru John Maeda told me, "Intuition is subconscious wis- dom. When it comes to business decisions, I want to combine intuition with data."

Biplab Sarkar, CEO of Vectorworks, echoed John, stating, "Intuition is what separates me from others. I think it is very important in the decision-making process—especially if your environment is changing. In engineering, the most important thing is timely decision-making. You must make the decision, and you must own it, learn from it, and go forward." Being attuned to his intuition helps Biplab to own his decisions.

In business it often takes guts to stand up for your intuition in the face of data and rationale. Deciding to listen to your heart is a brave—and often solitary—path. But interestingly, we do embrace the intuitive when it comes to machine intuition.

Scientists are spending an inordinate amount of time building up the intuitive capacity of machines, yet we ignore our own inherent intuitive strengths and capacity.

Think of leading with intuition as three concentric circles. Wonder is at the core because stillness and observation are required for us to hear that little voice inside. The second circle is discernment—finding the strength to act on our intuition and speak up. Rigor often comes into play here as we dig deep to find the data to back up our intuition. The outermost circle comes from making a practice of listening to and acting on our intuition. This is the point at which intuition becomes an essential tool in our leadership tool kit. As Kelley Black, founder and CEO of Balancing the Executive Life, put it, "The rational mind can be self-limiting. We need to normalize the intuitive in leadership. Intuition in leadership is critical because it helps you see a broader field."

Intuition helps us lead with our whole selves—creatively and strategically.

INTUITION IS A DATA POINT

What if we started acknowledging that intuition is a kind of data? Amanda Potter, designer for Fitler Club, framed it as "using memory beyond the quantifiable." Matt Vander Laan, head of corporate communications at MonoSol, manufacturer of a water-soluble film for packing goods, explained, "Intuition is drawing from a library of experience. You must be looking for patterns to break patterns." As I mentioned in the previous chapter, intuition is also sort of like improvising with yourself. At least, that is how it played out for Zumba cofounder Alberto "Beto" Pérez.

Imagine a phenomenon of gyrating bodies moving in sync to salsa, reggaeton, and house music. Imagine it on the White House lawn, spearheaded by former first lady Michelle Obama; on the subzero terrain of Antarctica; in community centers at housing projects in some of our most blighted cities; and at sunset on pristine Hawaiian beaches. This phenomenon is Zumba, a dance exercise platform that has launched thousands of instructors into entrepreneurship and changed millions of people's lives. It started with a hunch from cofounders Beto Pérez and Alberto Perlman.

Intuition is inherent to Zumba dance moves and part of its origin story. Back in the 1990s, Beto was a choreographer and dance instructor. He had forgotten his exercise routine book before a class he was about to teach. And so he challenged himself to improvise a 20-minute routine to salsa music with steps that were intuitive and easy to follow. It was a huge hit.

In 2001, joined by third partner Alberto Aghion, Beto and Alberto Perlman asked themselves a big question: "What if we take our last $14,000 and offer instructors and followers a way to be trained [in Zumba] and ways to stay connected to build a community?" Acting on their intuition, they hit "Send" on an email seeking Zumba instructors. They hoped to receive 200 responses and they got 450 . . . in the first hour.

Zumba is based on two principles:

1. Fun creates everlasting behavioral change.

2. Dance brings people together.

The founders banked on their hunch that people would respond to the following fitness model: Dance + Exercise + Sweat = Smiles. Consider that this was during a time when dance was either in the domain of nightclubs or on concert stages, and the main sound resounding through gyms was the crashing of dumbbells on rubber-covered floors—not salsa or house music. We forget that before Zumba, there was a big separation between sweaty bodies and smiling faces—never the two did meet. Today, we take this combination for granted, and we have Zumba to thank. In fact, the Zumba community has a mnemonic—FEJ, or "freeing, electrifying joy"—to describe the intuitive release and spontaneity that happens for participants in every class.

Today, there are more locations teaching Zumba than there are McDonald's restaurants in the world. Zumba is a multimillion-dollar business in 186 countries and more than 200,000 gyms, with 15 million people using it as their principal form of exercise. In 2006, it pivoted to an instructor-centered business model and rocketed to 40,000 percent revenue growth.

While we don't teach MBA students to practice listening to their intuition in business school, every successful entrepreneur references it. Entrepreneurs take intuition very seriously. This is evident in the origin stories of successful start-up leaders like Beto Pérez. When they share how they got started, there is always a moment when they say a variation of the following: "Something told me not to do the deal" or "Something told me to work with her over him even though her pedigree wasn't as impressive." That something is intuition.

Lily Fischer and Nima Etemadi, cofounders of Cake Life Bake Shop in Philadelphia, credit intuition not only for bringing them together but also for getting them out of a nerve-racking business deal that would have pushed them into growing at an uncomfortable clip. Ben Batory, a senior vice president at Franklin Templeton Investments, talks about the ways he has used a combination of his intuition and experiential knowledge to make decisions at the trading desk in his career. Steve Jobs paid homage to intuition when he said, "Intuition is a very powerful thing, more powerful than intellect, in my opinion. That's had a big impact on my work."[3]

What do all of these successful leaders have in common? They take stock of intuitive moments as data points and internal alerts. They leverage their ability to unconsciously recognize patterns as a strategic tool.

INTUITION AND WICKED PROBLEMS

When the US military entered Afghanistan in 2001, they found the terrain to be volatile, uncertain, complex, and ambiguous (for obvious reasons). Thus was born the acronym *VUCA*, first coined by the US Army War College in Carlisle, Pennsylvania. Soon thereafter, corporate America began adopting the VUCA term to describe the turbulent market environments that companies have to survive and navigate. We must become comfortable with ambiguity because it is a real and present part of being human.

Ambiguity isn't going anywhere. Leaders are being required to get more comfortable with abstractions and "unknown unknowns"—that is, not knowing what they don't know. Markets are imperfect, inconsistent, and unpredictable because they are made of imperfect, inconsistent, and unpredictable people. Wicked problems abound in our VUCA world. They are those complex quandaries such as income disparity, global lack of access to potable water, and terrorism. There are no linear and straightforward answers to these challenges. They are gnarly and ambiguous, and require us to think like systems designers.

A wicked problem is one that requires abductive reasoning, whereby you start with a set of information and try to get to logical, plausible (but not definitive) explanations for those observations. In the abductive process, you have incomplete puzzle pieces—they could be a combination of quantitative data points as well as observations—and then you reach the likeliest conclusion. Physicians do this with diagnoses; they never have a complete picture, just a myriad of data points, such as a consult with the patient, lab reports, and conversations with colleagues.

Claude Silver, the chief heart officer at VaynerMedia, told me that she is a strategic systems thinker who feels her way around the world and operates on gut: "In any given meeting I am using a myriad of tools and inquiry that seem relevant for that situation." She extends the metaphor of the heart as the central operating system in the body to people being the central operating system in organizations.

In VUCA environments, where data is limited and wicked problems are everywhere, embracing abductive reasoning and your intuition is necessary. In fact, intuition is often how you make the leap from observation to plausible explanation. It begins with the stillness that observation and curiosity require. It leads to clearing out the clutter and bravely following our hearts.

INTUITION PUTS BRAVERY BEFORE MASTERY

The film *Hearts Beat Loud* is a story about a father (Frank) and daughter (Sam) bonding through their love of music. During a phase of self-doubt, Sam's girlfriend Rose declares words of encouragement to her: "You gotta be brave before you can be good." Likewise, intuition goads us on into bravery before mastery. It serves as a flashlight, guiding us through the dimly lit tunnel of unknown terrain as we make our way out into clarity.

Being brave before being masterful is a leap—a leap into trusting our intuition. The first result is that you become an astute recognizer of patterns. This attunement to your surroundings gives you a real distillation of next steps. The second result is that you reduce regret. There's nothing worse than having known something beyond the rational but then going in a different direction.

In business it often takes guts to stand up for your intuition in the face of data and rationale. Deciding to listen to your heart is a brave—and often solitary—path. Gaining the stamina and endurance to follow that path requires that you cultivate your intuitive core. Grammy-nominated DJ King Britt cultivates his by traveling because it is in those foreign situations when you are less familiar with your surroundings that you must rely on your inner sense. Stillness also helps, because it prompts us to be better observers, to be more curious, and to become active listeners.

The paradox of intuition is that as internal a process as it is, it consistently requires us to pay deep attention to the world around us. Ultimately, it helps us to get outside of ourselves and span boundaries. Boundary spanning is extremely important in the future of learning as well as in the future of work. It is the ability to bridge chasms and gaps to have conversations across disciplines and to connect silos. Boundary spanning is also extremely important in building a community where creativity can thrive, as we will explore in the next chapter.

 CREATIVITY LEAP EXERCISE

FOR YOU
► Reflect on and journal about all of the times you have followed your heart. What was the result? Gain courage from this. Journaling the way you have historically followed your intuition will become a documentation and memory bank of your intuitive leaps.

FOR YOUR ORGANIZATION
► Hold weekly Wonder Sprints. A Wonder Sprint is a designated amount of time when your team does a deep dive into an exploratory and audacious question. The best question prompts for a Wonder Sprint start with "What if . . . ?" It should indicate what your organization intuits and anticipates is around the corner in terms of trends or moves the competition will make. Design them as short as 15 minutes or as long as a half day. Choose an interesting prompt ("What if we partnered with our biggest competitor?"), or hold it in a playful environment, like a bowling alley.

CHAPTER 6

COMMUNE
COME TOGETHER TO CREATE

TRIBES ARE THE FOUNDATION
FOR CREATIVE COMMUNITY

When I was growing up in the northwest section of Philadelphia, in the Mount Airy neighborhood, the kids on my street and one block over formed a tribe. We had roles. We knew where each other stood in the pecking order, and we created our own rituals, artifacts, and space for playing tag and hopscotch, jumping Double Dutch, and knowing whose front stoop we could or could not hang out on.

What made our tribe work was that all of our distinctive personalities were complementary. Our quirky differences were accepted and allowed to sparkle depending on what was at stake and at play. This helped our own unique personalities develop a distinctive edge. We were also uncannily aware if some kid from a different block—a foreigner—sent over to sniff things out and possibly disturb our flow was *not* a part of our tribe. Sometimes we bumped into these foreigners on the three-block walk to the corner store to buy a nickel bag of "Swedish fish" candy. We had to make a decision as to whether the newer entrant would be friend or foe.

Fast-forward decades later. At 8:30 on Sunday mornings I show up at DanceFit to begin my ritual of a thorough stretch class, followed by a vibrant, sweaty, booty-shaking hip-hop dance class. It is a form of restoration and renewal for me. What most excites me about these classes is that they are my way of getting back into my dance tribe.

I grew up studying dance, but it was difficult to keep up after college. If you're not trying to audition for a Broadway show, there are few options between advanced-beginner classes for 11-year-old kids and classes for professional dancers in their 20s. Discovering DanceFit has been a lifesaver; it's a place that reconnects me to a part of myself. Simultaneously, I also started taking social dance lessons in the foxtrot and salsa at the Society Hill Dance Academy, where years ago I also studied tango. I was lucky enough to find two dance tribes.

Tribes are subsets of community. In Seth Godin's book *Tribes: We Need You to Lead Us*, we learn that tribes are an outgrowth of our human instinct to unite. They are forces for change and influence. Tribes are both safe havens and a survival mechanism. They are a means to an end when it comes to building affinity, and they also jumpstart the momentum needed to quickly accomplish things like "Run for the hills, we're being attacked!" They prioritize and preserve what matters (such as language and rituals) in times of complexity.[1]

I reference tribes because I believe that a sense of community and the ability to work together toward a common goal are essential to creativity. Community is the ideal space in which wonder and rigor can thrive.

WHY COMMUNITY IS ESSENTIAL
FOR CREATIVITY

It is hard to go it alone when generating something new. It helps to have the right team around you. The Steelcase study discussed in chapter 1 reported that for 90 percent of respondents, collaboration was essential to create new and better ideas. And research from the Institute for Corporate Productivity shows that profitability increases when people collaborate. That is because it is difficult to sustain a creative practice on our own. Community is a force more powerful than ourselves that can recharge and reorient us to continue the fundamentals of inquiring, improvising, and intuiting.

It is through the shared experiences in community that wonder and rigor get amplified. But as in any dynamic effort, there are both advantages and challenges in community. One advantage is the boundary spanning, the bridge building, that occurs when we connect with people different from us (albeit bonded by similar goals). A trust in what we have in common helps us to stretch and reach beyond what we initially see and assume about others. That connection to something larger than ourselves forces us to find common ground. Community is the place and state of mind whereby, despite our differences, we are at one.

But the same comfort that makes you feel so rock-solid can also inadvertently divide. We see this often in the increasingly nationalist political climate around the world, where people hold fast to their beliefs to protect themselves from "the other," no matter if it makes rational sense and even if all the data points otherwise. This reality exposes the fact that it takes work to preserve healthy community. While tribes are the foundation for creative community, if we leave the creative process only to incubate in tribes, we risk falling into an echo chamber trap. Tribal thinking can be divisive.

Sustaining community is a brave balancing act. Taking advantage of its attributes (boundary spanning, fostering empathy, sparking curiosity because of innate differences) must be done in the midst of mitigating its challenges. Community is messy. The challenges of community require rigor to resolve. To be in community takes effort, reconciliation, and the creative abrasion referenced in chapter 3. Communities consist of tribes bumping up against each other, with their own agendas, proclivities, and techniques to get things done. Even in the most well-designed community, we must be vigilant to ensure diversity, avoid groupthink, and resist settling for the status quo. This is where practicing inquiry, improvisation, and intuition is essential—so that we have the space to adapt, grow, and take creativity leaps.

DESIGNING COMMUNITY FOR CREATIVITY

To get a sense of how organizations design communities for creativity, I visited NASA's Jet Propulsion Lab (JPL) in Pasadena, California. The Studio at JPL is its built-in instigator. It helps spark creativity for JPL's community of scientists. It is led by Visual Strategist Daniel Goods and is staffed by a multidisciplinary group of social scientists, artists, and designers.

"The Studio helps the scientists explain, 'Here's why you should care about this thing I'm working on,'" Daniel told me. With the Studio's assistance, JPL scientists can tell the story of their research in tangible, visual, and compelling ways. One example is the *Line of Sight* installation[2] on the JPL campus. It features three rotating LED signs that orient to planets and other celestial bodies in space. It has become a physical and visual cue on the JPL campus of NASA's mission. It also illustrates the value for a community to have a built-in provocateur for creativity. Without these provocations from the Studio to explain their work, scientists risk going unchallenged in translating and communicating their efforts.

Another example I found of building in provocation in a work community is at the software company Autodesk, where they intentionally build teams that span boundaries. Randy Swearer, VP of learning futures, explained,

> In a world where the software is updating every few weeks, the sectors it is applied in are transforming at astonishing rates, and the associated professional roles are morphing too, then learning becomes everything. Our team's job is to help Autodesk imagine futures out of this complexity: What kind of research will we need? What kind of business model? What kinds of issues are our customers facing? What new values are they trying to create?

Randy believes this work is best done by having people from totally different backgrounds jointly examine scenarios. For example, an Autodesk team might include coders, a person with a PhD in anthropology, and a former military general. In addition to forming diverse teams internally, Randy's team hosts Summit Series, in which they reach out to strategic partners and convene diverse thought leaders and practitioners from around the world to focus on a theme that is important to Autodesk.

> Creativity is a group enterprise here. We spend a lot of time and money to teach people how to work in teams, using different roles, using different intelligences on teams to create that creative collective brain. That's predominantly the way we work here because the big things happen on teams.

Autodesk's cognitively diverse internal teams and external outreach through their Summit Series are examples of creative abrasion we discussed in chapter 3. They also point out how dynamic and far-reaching collaborative community building needs to be to spark creativity.

ZOOM IN, ZOOM OUT

When you walk into Chocolat Abeille in Omaha, Nebraska, you have a palpable sense that you have just stepped into someone's space of peace. Tina Tweedy, the proprietor, is a friendly and bright-eyed chocolatier. It was only after I was paying for my dark chocolate almond brittle that I noticed the photograph of Tina in a white beekeeper's outfit. I asked her about the photograph, and her face lit up. She went on to describe the joy that beekeeping brings her. She explained to me that many of her chocolates are infused with honey from her bees. Then I observed that the wallpaper in the chocolate boutique was decorated with delicately etched bees in gold metallic paint.

Bees are spectacular teachers for understanding creativity. This is because beehives are chaordic communities. To me, at first glance a beehive looks like a throbbing mess. There is wax dangling off the newly constructed edges of the hive cells, and bees appear to be clustered in random areas. But upon closer inspection I observe incredible amounts of wonder and rigor. The hexagonal cells are on consistent repeat; the bees form clusters with their own mathematical intuition; and each bee is intentionally occupied, working in its own way to ensure that the queen can give birth to more bees. The hive is both one and many, each individual bee existing for the sole purpose of the community. Tina agreed with my take on beehives and that her work as a chocolatier needs the chaos (and wonder) and order (and rigor) working together beautifully to create magic.

> Play, for me, is every day. For example, last weekend I decided to make chocolate flamingoes; people loved that. Having that element of play makes my work enjoyable. And constraints drive me. [For example,] to store my chocolate, I use a wine cooler. I didn't want to pay the thousands of dollars for the technically correct cooler when a wine cooler has the same humidity controls.

I learned even more about creativity and bees from two other beekeepers, Norris Childs and Randy Frederick. Did you know that bees know exactly what they are doing and for how long, whether they are worker bees (i.e., female bees) or drone bees (i.e., male honeybees)? And did you know that the queen bee is the leader in name only? She isn't really in charge. It is the female worker bees—which are either cleaners or nurses—who direct the queen as to which type of larva to lay. They also decide when it is time to leave and make a new hive.

Swarming happens when a bee community detects that it needs to divide and make a new hive. The bees' swarming function is a great example of complexity at work; it is self-organizing, adaptive, and emergent. To decide when to swarm, the worker bees make sense out of a number of variables, including storage room for honey, time of year, temperature in the hive, and a sense of whether the hive is too crowded or too sparse.

When the hive splits, half of the bees remain in the original honeycomb, and half of the bees fly out the hive, find a new tree branch, and surround the queen bee to keep her warm, at precisely 95 degrees Fahrenheit. To create a new hive, the bees must come to a unanimous decision. They debate back and forth, scout out new spaces, and measure the space by forming a chain of bees to determine width and height. The entrance must be large enough to fly into but small enough so that mice and other critters cannot enter.

Observing bee communities at work reminds me of how important it is to zoom in on rigorous details but also zoom out to experience the wonder of community. This is sense-making brought to an entirely new level. Imagine if our human organizations were able to make decisions in such democratic ways, balancing out mathematical precision and intuition. As beekeeper John Childs observed, "The chaos is our perception of bees' order. Every bee knows what it is doing."

What is very much going on in bee communities as you zoom in is random self-organization, adapting to the needs of the community in the moment. As you zoom out, you see a full picture of emergence. And zooming out to gain perspective is exactly what we need to do to forecast and creatively prepare for what is to come, as we will explore next.

 CREATIVITY LEAP EXERCISE

FOR YOU

► Rituals institute order and rigor into our lives, often with wondrous outcomes. What is a personal ritual you could create for yourself to feel more connected to your work community? It could be a salutation you say to yourself upon entering the lobby; it could be an object you reference at your desk; or it could be a quick daily walk around the office floor quietly observing your colleagues and absorbing what they contribute. Check out *Rituals for Work: 50 Ways to Create Engagement, Shared Purpose, and a Culture That Can Adapt to Change*, by Kursat Ozenc and Margaret Hagan, for more ideas.

FOR YOUR ORGANIZATION

► One way to build community at work is to honor institutional memory. Make the time to take stock of where you have been as an organization. Do as Matt Vander Laan of MonoSol did and curate and convene a company show and tell that highlights projects showcasing "where we've been." Highlight the people responsible for initiating the ideas. Make sure you ask a diverse group of people throughout the organization to lead in the storytelling so that you share out diverse perspectives.

CHAPTER 7

FORECAST
AMPLIFY WHAT IS UNIQUELY HUMAN

THE FUTURE OF THE WORLD
DEPENDS ON CREATIVITY

During the summer of 2018, when I met Julian Harzheim (from chapter 1) in Shenzhen, I also reconnected with Mart Maasik. One morning, Mart and I caught up over breakfast because we hadn't seen each other in several years. Mart is Estonian and spends a lot of his working days just across the Baltic Sea in Stockholm, Sweden. He is cofounder of the Innovation Lab at SEB Bank, a leading partnership bank in Northern Europe. At one point he casually referenced "the chip in my hand."

Thinking I hadn't heard him correctly, I asked, "Wait, did you just say you have a chip in your hand?" He nodded in the affirmative and went on to explain that the SEB Innovation Lab decided they needed to act out innovation, not just have the word "Innovation" in their title. They began hosting "Beer & Chips" parties after work where various colleagues opted in for a tattoo artist to inject a microchip the size of a grain of rice into the fleshy part of the hand at the base of the thumb.

"Can I feel it?" I asked Mart. "Sure," he responded. I touched what felt like a tiny bone spur. Mart explained that he was not an early adopter but actually a laggard in the grand scheme of things. Now that he has one, he enjoys using the chip to gain easy access to his office building and to unlock his bicycle. He told me that he might use it for mass transit.

I was gobsmacked. I felt like a Luddite. Hearing Mart's story was correlating well to many of my daily experiences in Shenzhen. Every day, I observed a virtually cashless society— all exchange for goods and services was being done by scanning QR codes on smartphones. And there I thought I was cutting-edge back home in the United States because I paid for groceries with the Apple Pay app on my iPhone. Mart's chip caused me to think about how political economies have a cultural context. To what extent was my very American affinity for privacy and individualism making me and other Americans more reticent about adopting such technology?

Many times when I tell the story of Mart and the chip in his hand, people gasp, clutch their own hands, and have a look of horror. Granted, these are mostly Americans, but the point is that Mart's story is a cautionary tale about adapting to new shifts.

The fourth industrial revolution (4IR) is here. Ubiquitous cloud technology, automation of tasks in both white collar and blue collar work, artificial intelligence (AI), virtual reality (VR), and augmented reality (AR)—the preponderance of digital and soon quantum platforms are all part of daily life. History shows that rarely are we prepared for the leaps that each industrial revolution presents to us. So what can we do to adapt to this one? How can we forecast what will be needed to survive and thrive in this new frontier of ubiquitous technology?

Perspective is a loaded oxymoron. We need it to forge ahead, yet it can only be gained from past experience. Perspective is about mining from the past in order to get insight into the future. Forecasting is about mining those insights in order to anticipate and identify multiple possible futures so that we can adapt to bumps in the road. To that end, forecasting requires a practice of inquiry, improvisation, and intuition; it necessitates an ability to toggle between wonder and rigor. In short, forecasting and preparing for what is to come requires creativity.

Creativity drives us to produce variations on the old and design ready-made experiments for anticipated future states. It matters more than ever because it offers us a way to be adaptive to increasing rates of change. Len Damico, head of design at software design and product development company Arcweb Technologies, agrees. He believes that society's less ambiguous problems will likely be left for machine learning and artificial intelligence. But for the increasing number of fuzzy, ambiguous, nonroutine stuff, for our wicked problems like college debt forgiveness or gentrification and displacement in American cities, we will need to leverage our creativity to solve them. And as Paul Petrone, head of academic and government marketing at LinkedIn Learning, wrote, "While robots are great at optimizing old ideas, organizations most need creative employees who can conceive the solutions of tomorrow."

CREATIVITY IN THE FOURTH INDUSTRIAL REVOLUTION

The first industrial revolution (1760–1840) was about transitioning from hand production to machine production through steam and water technology. The second (1880s–1920s) was the age of mass production, when standardization and electrification were introduced into manufacturing. The automotive and apparel production industries were greatly impacted. The third industrial revolution (1950s–1990s) basically varied the scale and scope of manufacturing through digitized manufacturing and mass customization. In the three prior industrial revolutions, humans typically have merged into the technology, not the other way around. Take the 1936 Charlie Chaplin film *Modern Times*, when Chaplin is ultimately swallowed up by the cogs and wheels of the factory machine.

Galit Ariel, a technofuturist and an immersive tech expert, insists that there are opportunities in this fourth industrial revolution to use technology to amplify what is uniquely human about us. Humans and technology have the opportunity to coexist in this 4IR. In one of her *Futurithmic* articles, Galit encouraged tech creators to generate human-centric solutions where we would coexist with technology. Robots should be thought of as "automated colleagues." Galit sees lots of opportunity for creativity to be amplified with AR:

> I love the term "augmented reality" because it describes exactly how this technology could be groundbreaking. It will enable us to amplify and interact with the physical world and with technology in new ways. AR would literally transform the physical world around us into a three-dimensional canvas, where we can paint digital experiences around us. We will start touching again and looking at surfaces in new ways. We'll be able to amplify, enhance, and explore the world and our senses in new ways—mixing visual, sonic, tactile, and olfactory with digital interactions.[1]

In Galit's view, the future will provide ways to intersect with technology through a range of our senses, opening new ways to explore our creativity.

Balder Onarheim is a creativity neuroscientist and president of PlatoScience. With a background in medical equipment engineering, he has landed on a similar solution for how humans can adapt to the fourth industrial revolution. In a 2017

Emerging Technologies Tech France talk, he proposed that we have been asking the wrong questions of artificial intelligence.[2] Instead of wondering how to make AI creative, we should be asking, "How might we combine the calculating power of AI with the creative power of the human brain?" Instead of trying to make AI creative, let's explore how we can link humans' innate creativity with AI. That, to Balder, is the more interesting and relevant question. For both Galit and Balder, human creativity is at the core of what makes us unique and distinct from machines, robots, and computers—and the key to taking advantage of this ubiquitous technology is upping the ante on what makes us uniquely human.

In order to leverage our creativity in this fourth industrial revolution, Heather McGowan, a future of work strategist, has called for a shift away from learning to work and toward working to learn. In other words, the future of work is the future of learning. I predict that this new "working to learn" orientation will bring about a return to the apprenticeship model, one that engages people from a range of ages in on-the-job experiential learning. It is emblematic of what economists Deirdre McCloskey and Brad DeLong have discussed in their research: that the future of work will be more about decision-making, critical thinking, and providing human connection and less about rote implementation.

The signs of this impending shift are already here. In two critically acclaimed television shows, *Black-ish* and *Big Little Lies*, teenage characters reject the expectation that they will go straight from high school to college. In the case of *Black-ish*, Junior insists that he wants to take a gap year, and in *Big Little Lies*, Abigail declares that she won't even apply to college because she has already taken a job with a start-up. These characters reflect a centennial generation (also called Generation Z) that questions the ROI of a college education and wants more

hands-on learning—the kind of learning that requires a practice
of inquiry, improvisation, and intuition to continually level up.

PREPARING ORGANIZATIONS FOR THE FUTURE

The best way for an organization to increase its creativity quotient for the future is by getting the right, diverse set of people
in the room. Thought diversity moves us away from only valuing deep specialization to spanning boundaries. This helps us
to cultivate communities of creative thinkers. Thought diversity
is often an overlooked area, especially for companies that are
established and may suffer from a superiority complex. A superiority complex and a too-big-to-fail attitude can make them
complacent, putting them at a huge disadvantage. Proactively
seeking out thought diversity means that you cannot recruit
from the usual suspects of organizations. Emergent leaders
will not be found in the most obvious places. Sometimes they
are embedded deep within and are more valuable because they
gather different types of insights due to their perspective. But
they could also be your newest hires or come from completely
different industries and backgrounds. It is their perspective and
the ways that they frame questions, adapt on the fly, and act on
their intuition that count.

As companies develop a culture of creativity, they will begin
embracing new and integrative work processes from previously
unexplored realms—for example, from fashion, jazz, dance,
and, yes, even farming. Farmers are the original hackers.

Gary and Amy Manoff own a five-acre fruit farm in New
Hope, Pennsylvania. Every season they need to figure out what
more they can do with the peaches and apples they harvest.
While the VUCA environment that corporate America deals
with can be a beast, the earth that the Manoffs must contend
with is a far greater one. It is loaded with uncertainty and
ambiguity.

Not everyone is cut out to be a farmer. Gary refers to the farming bug as a disease; either you've got it or you don't. When I visited the Manoff Market Gardens and Cidery, they showed me their latest creativity leap: a cidery. It was born out of their constant exploration of "What's next?" Amy has taken inspiration from the *Cheaper by the Dozen* story. She loved the way the Gilbreth family of 12 kids and two adults were essentially efficiency experts. As a result, she is driven by the question "How might we make this job easier, faster, and better?"

> I do not want to waste. I got all these squishy peaches; we have to do something with them! Butters, jams, jellies, vinegars, and ciders. As a small farm, it is hard to get efficiencies.
>
> Four years ago, Gary had been reading and researching, and he brought home these ciders. We started drinking them, and I thought, "What is this?" And so we began pressing our own cider, and it was nothing special at first. We started including staff in our cider tastings at the end of the day and would ask them, "What do you taste? What does it do for you?" We did this for a couple of years.
>
> Gary was really driven. He had vision. He said, "I want to make cider the proper way." We ended up going on a cider producers trip. We learned that each farm used what they had to make a traditional cider. All used apples, barrels, and yeast that were available where they lived. It was a very important learning. So we had to go back to being creative and open to explore the opportunity. By stepping back and doing something no one else was doing, we had to ask ourselves, "What do we have here that's unique, and how can we make it delicious?"

This story is the perfect example of how a creativity leap can occur. First came the wonder of tasting cider. Then came the big questions: Why don't we create our own cider so that we can have a new product and be more efficient? What do we need to know about the cider-making process? How can we make it delicious? And through a rigorous process of improvisation and iterative tinkering, the Manoffs landed on their own process for making cider that intuitively feels right to them. We may never farm a day in our lives, yet there is so much to learn from farmers like Gary and Amy.

As Bhushan Sethi, joint global leader of PwC's People & Organization practice, told me, "Everyone is introducing technology as the productivity play, but we must upskill people and manage their fears and burnout, and redesign the ways work gets done." *Upskilling* refers to teaching employees new technology skills so that they can evolve their role. *Reskilling* means to take on completely new roles. There is lots of anxiety with reskilling. Bringing people along to reskill them for adjacent roles requires that an organization be transparent and purpose driven and think in terms of entirely new business models— much as the Manoffs have done. Bhushan cautions,

> If we are not transparent, and create a narrative internally, then folks will draw conclusions, look for other roles, and invest in their own learning. Or produce worse anxiety among their colleagues. A whisper-down-the-lane effect could result in organizational populism. In the end, all of us will need learning agility skills.

Creativity is about challenging our assumptions about what the "right way" or "best way" is to do things. It is how we test out new ways of being and doing to prepare for an uncertain and ambiguous future. So what happens when we just go on autopilot, not acknowledging that there could be better ways to do things? Take meetings, for example. Meetings are notoriously bad at engaging a wide range of people and going beyond the traditional reporting-out model. There is a lot to be gained by creatively disrupting where meetings take place, their duration, who leads them, and their frequency. We could begin by conducting walking or standing meetings. As humans, we are designed to move. The spinal cord is an extension of the medulla oblongata at the base of the brain. When we sit for long periods of time hunched over our computer, we cut off blood and oxygen supply to our brain. We actually do think better on our feet! The US Navy has had standing meetings for decades. People get to the point a lot faster, and meetings are succinct.

It is also becoming popular to take calls while walking outside. Why not opt for a change of scenery by going on a walk in nature to hash out the details of a matter or to think more expansively about pressing issues? More opportunities for "activity-based work" (or ABW) are popping up outside of the traditional work environment. Take, for example, Fitler Club, a private stay/work/play concept club in Philadelphia. David Gutstadt founded it to foster organic connections: "It's the Marie Kondo model—to make life simpler. People's lives are complicated. Despite our fixation on devices, people still crave connections and want to be where there are other like-minded people."

What if more corporations flipped the script, the cadence, and the space in which people worked? What new insights could result? Which newly energized employees would show up?

This is exactly the experiment that Arcweb Technologies is trying. Arcweb is based in the Old City neighborhood of Phil-adelphia. I met with Len Damico, head of design, and James Koran, principal consultant, about the firm's decision to move to an asynchronous work schedule: staff work from home two days a week and in the office three days a week. I was curious to understand how it was affecting productivity. They both affirmed that "the days we are remote are the most productive days." Len said that on the days he is out of the office, he can do deep work and then talk about the work with colleagues the next day. "When I am here, it is harder to get into that deep thought space. When I return, it feels like it's humming here," he said.

I call their new work cadence a type of organizational peristalsis. If you remember your basic human biology, then you recall that for chewed-up food to go from our mouth to our stomach, it must travel first through the esophagus. The esophagus has an involuntary muscle system that squeezes and releases food, a process called peristalsis. Similarly, Arcweb's testing out asynchronous work is a kind of organizational peristalsis. They are allowing for a squeezing and release of pressure points, for moments of working solo and together, for the wonder and rigor that creativity necessitates. James said,

> If I have crazy ideas, typically I would bring others in. Now I disrupt my team less. I take a step back and write it down. It forces me to get the abstract ideas out of my head and into a sketch outline. The next day I might think it's a horrible idea. . . . It slows me down and ultimately speeds up my team.

A great learning for Arcweb's leadership by working in this ebb-and-flow cadence is that the relationship between time spent on a project and output is nonlinear. As James put it, "The work is not matchy-matchy. It is slough, breakthrough, pivot, slough, breakthrough. And then, I guess, we are done." They have found that their new work process strips away the biases that could be noise so that they can more clearly focus on the signals.

HYBRID THINKERS WELCOME

There are two competing narratives about the future of work. In the midst of the fourth industrial revolution we have painted a picture of ubiquitous automation, cloud technology, virtual and augmented reality, and artificial intelligence in competition with humans. Our dystopian narrative says, "Run for the hills! The robots are taking over!" But our other, more utopian, narrative says to chill out; not much will change in the aggregate. People who do lose their jobs to robots will simply retrain and be reeducated for different sorts of jobs. I believe the truth is somewhere in the middle, a hybrid of both perspectives. Ira Kalish, chief global economist at Deloitte, agrees. He explained to me, "In the short term, people will be displaced. But history tells us that the winners outnumber the losers and more new jobs will be created."

An either/or, love-hate approach to technology and the increasing ambiguity in our world is simply not viable. To create hybrid solutions that use technology to amplify what is uniquely human about us and prepare us to solve tomorrow's problems, we need to be hybrid thinkers.

Technology is nothing without human inputs. As Shelly Palmer, a musician and technology consultant, said in a 2017 interview in *strategy+business*, "To get the most out of an algorithm, you must ask the right questions. . . . Cognitive non-repetitive tasks . . . are [hard] to replicate."[3] What our future world needs is more creative, hybrid thinkers who are asking the big blue-sky questions about what technology can do for us and are also willing to undergo the rigor to find those answers.

CREATIVITY LEAP EXERCISE

FOR YOU
▸ Watch Balder Onarheim's TEDxCopenhagen talk on the neuroscience of creativity. Try one of his tips at the end. For example, while brushing your teeth, practice stringing along as many words as possible through random association. For example, how many randomly associated words can you come up with after thinking of the word "airplane"?

FOR YOUR ORGANIZATION
▸ Switch up the way you hold meetings to see what emerges. Change the environment: go outside. Or change the structure: ask a junior employee to lead the meeting, in his or her own way.

CHAPTER 8

REMIX, REFRAME, REPURPOSE

THERE IS NOTHING NEW UNDER THE SUN

Originality is a steep expectation. While toggling between
wonder and rigor leads to the new and the novel, originality
depends on context. Being creative on an intentional basis
might be a less threatening endeavor if we allowed ourselves to
accept that we are regularly borrowing from one another, ourselves, our histories, and different adjacent cultures. Creativity
is about the remix: repurposing, recombining, and reframing.

Creativity requires you to reexamine what is right in front
of you and internally mine it for new ideas. Or . . . you can look
externally and, in the words of author Austin Kleon, "steal
like an artist."[1] Originality is not the result of a purist singular
production. Rather, it is the product of common memes that are
consistent temporally and spatially throughout the world. Originality, one can argue, is not even an actual thing in creativity.
This in fact is what Michael Chabon, a Pulitzer Prize–winning
American novelist and short-story writer, asserts in David
Eagleman's documentary *The Creative Brain*. The plotlines and
characters in his novels play on variations of the archetypal

plots of stories that have been with humans for centuries. There is no shame in Chabon's game. To him, originality is a product of reinvention through remixing what has come before. He embraces the challenge of finding the patterns that speak to him, reinterpreting them, and building on them.

ARCHETYPES ARE PATTERNS

Archetypes underscore this idea that originality is a misnomer. One of Carl Jung's biggest contributions to the fields of psychology, anthropology, and sociology was to outline universal archetypes that are part of the collective unconscious. Archetypes are patterns. They repeat themselves around the world regardless of culture, century, gender, geography, or language. These age-old memes reappear globally in stories, mythology, religion, art, and dreams. We respond to them viscerally. The 12 basic archetypes listed in *The Hero and the Outlaw: Building Extraordinary Brands Through the Power of Archetypes*, by Margaret Mark and Carolyn Pearson, are as follows:

1. *Caregiver.* Compassionate and a martyr; helps with doing for others.
2. *Creator.* Imaginative and artistic; helps with realizing a vision.
3. *Everyman.* Empathic, accessible, down to earth; helps with belonging.
4. *Explorer.* Freedom and autonomy; helps with experiencing new things.
5. *Hero.* Courageous and competent, helps with improving the world.
6. *Innocent.* Freedom, traditional, and utopian; helps with doing things correctly.
7. *Jester.* Playful and lives in the moment; helps with lightening up the current environment.

8. *Lover.* Passionate and committed; helps with building connection to others.

9. *Magician.* Catalyst, inventive, and visionary; helps make dreams come true.

10. *Outlaw.* Rebellious and overturns what's dysfunctional; helps with disruption.

11. *Ruler.* Responsible, leadership; helps with creating prosperity.

12. *Sage.* Wise, intelligent; helps with explaining and analysis.[2]

In *The Hero and the Outlaw,* Mark and Pearson demonstrate the efficacy of borrowing from and using archetypes as a launchpad to create something novel and new. When brands incorporate archetypes effectively in their messaging, the ads touch us viscerally. Through metaphor and lateral thinking, archetypes help brand managers think through a problem and sell products on the level of human connection.

Integrating archetypes generates meaning that goes beyond a product's core functionality and usability. This is because a customer's long-term bond with a brand is based on the emotions it evokes and the experience it provides. Take Dove, for example. The focus of the "Real Beauty" campaign was less about soap and more about women's self-perception of beauty. Dove was not the first soap to hit the supermarket shelves targeting women. However, it was the first to effectively incorporate the Everywoman archetype into its branding.

Those Dove Real Beauty Sketches videos—they're real tearjerkers. My eyes well up when I watch the women break down as they hear their natural beauty described to them through the lens of a stranger, based on sketches drawn by forensic artist Gil Zamora. I feel what those women are feeling. Similarly, Dove caught Oprah Winfrey's attention when they used real everywomen in their television commercials, replete with tummies, cellulite, soft curves, and stretch marks. Dove's originality came from asking new questions of themselves, about how they wanted to represent beauty. Ultimately, the brand went from Everyman status to Hero status.

Archetypes can also be applied as true norths to enable change management in companies. Imagine how many interesting variations for a new strategic direction you could produce by applying one or a combination of these archetypes. Inspiration appears in the midst of rigorously applying skill and craft. And as Pablo Picasso is quoted as saying, "Inspiration exists, but it has to find you working." Even Picasso's cubist art, which made such a splash in Europe, was inspired by African sculpture. His originality came from his creative interpretations of angles, shading, color, and woodwork that had existed centuries before in other cultures foreign to his own.

The reappearance of archetypes across different cultures and throughout time demonstrates that the sources for creative inspiration are part of a larger network. Acts of creativity connect us because they require us to look for bridges. This is true boundary spanning.

THINK LIKE A FASHION DESIGNER

When I worked in the fashion industry, I received consistent reactions when I answered the question "So, what do you do?" at cocktail parties. Typically, people gave either an excited nod, impressed that I worked in such a glamorous industry, or a dismissive glazing over of the eyes, bored that I worked in such a frivolous industry.

The fashion industry is neither glamorous nor frivolous, and people's range of enchantment with and dismissal of fashion is naive. As iconic fashion designer Coco Chanel famously remarked, "Fashion is not something that exists in dresses only. Fashion is in the sky, in the street; fashion has to do with ideas, the way we live, what is happening."

Fashion has both temporal and spatial dimensions. Temporally, it values history and what has come before, while testing the boundaries of the present by offering futuristic twists in outlandish runway shows and couture. Fashion is also uniquely positioned for the present. If it is too far in the past, then it is costume. And if it is too far in the future, then people don't get it and it will not sell. Spatially, fashion borrows from the street and from the elite, from what is local and from remote regions of the world. Fashion designers have tapped into the underground subcultures of hip-hop and punk as well as aspirational elite groups. Globally, fashion is a $2.4 trillion business, driven by logistics, technology, supply chain management, consumer insights, and aesthetics.

By looking through the lens of a fashion designer, an apparel manufacturer, or a knitting mill, you can creatively arrive at novel and innovative ways to approach any challenge with which you have been sullenly wrestling. It was when I worked directly in the factories in Sri Lanka and Portugal that I witnessed some of the most amazing moments of using wonder and rigor to solve problems. Engineers in yarn-spinning mills would combine their knowledge of yarn torque and tension with the desired hand that a visiting team of designers was trying to achieve. It was during these moments of synthesis that some of the most creative problem-solving was done for merchandise that landed in stores a mere four months later.

I've observed for some time that elements from the fashion industry diffuse out to other sectors. Similar to the premise of Everett Rogers's diffusion of innovation theory from 1962, fashion elements and concepts spread into a wide range of companies, get adopted, and result in new, novel, and innovative products, services, and experiences. For example, the W Hotels unashamedly poached from the fashion industry when searching for ways to keep their hotels fresh and relevant (an admirable initiative for a hotel chain that was already hip when it launched). In 2010, the hotel brand hired fashion industry veteran Amanda Ross and created an entirely new role for her: global fashion director. They realized that they needed the skill and expertise from a fashion doyenne to remain current and relevant. Ross was responsible for everything from selecting the waitstaff uniforms to literally accessorizing the properties. The W Hotels have continued to value fashion's influence. In 2017, they appointed supermodel Joan Smalls as their first global fashion innovator.

Around the time I started thinking about fashion diffusion, my version of Rogers's theory, I came across Johanna Blakley's 2010 TEDx USC Talk, "Lessons from Fashion's Free Culture."[3] In it, Johanna discussed fashion's knock-off culture, wherein a designer's newly launched collections are knocked off— unabashedly copied with minimal adjustments. This is completely legal, as apparel is considered a functional object and thus not subject to copyright or trademark law.

Johanna explained that, paradoxically, fashion's knock-off culture instigates an aggressive churn of innovation. You cannot afford to rest on your laurels when you know that as soon as you release a new idea, it will be copied. As a result, fashion designers are on a steady diet of consuming inspiration from all sorts of unlikely and alternative sources. To be inimitable is fashion's survival skill. And it's a great lesson for companies in other industries.

Given our similar stances on fashion's underappreciated influence, I reached out to Johanna. We ended up publishing an academic paper on "fashion thinking," which caught the attention of Valerie Jacobs, the chief insight and innovation officer at LPK, a global brand design and innovation agency.[4] It turned out that Valerie had created a fashion thinking practice to help LPK leverage what was unique about their clients' brands. Valerie, Johanna, and I loved the simpatico of our approaches and developed a fashion thinking framework for clients who needed a new way to creatively drive innovation for their businesses. We defined fashion thinking as "a creative approach to business strategy that utilizes the best practices from the fashion industry to harness the power of technology, story, experimentation, trends, and open sourcing to add meaning and value to the functional and experiential spheres of products and services." There are seven principles in fashion thinking. Each of them points to a unique way that the fashion industry solves problems.

1. *Style.* Style is a form of curation. As such, it is an important tool for branding. The boundary spanning that fashion is adept at makes it able to bundle looks in seamless ways. This gives cues that subtly synchronize a brand. For example, you know a Burberry billboard ad from blocks away.

2. *Built for speed.* Due to fashion's knock-off culture, it uses technology to read cues from the customers, gather insights, and master speed to market. The evolution of fast fashion is evidence of this.

3. *Trends.* Valerie Jacobs says that "trends are data from the future." New patterns of behavior in society and popular culture are indicators of future trends. Gathering data from the future requires keen observation, listening, and not taking subtle shifts for granted.

4. *Storytelling.* When fashion designers build a collection, they start with a story made of characters, needs, and desires. The best retail experiences, such as the Anthropologie brand, lead with story in order to engage customers and compel them to buy so that they take a piece of that story home with them.

5. *Two-way engagement.* Fashion firms understand that push marketing is passé and that a push-pull

conversation with consumers is ideal. Warby Parker embodied this when, in an early-stage marketing move, they traveled to potential customers in a yellow school bus, showcasing their eyewear. They understood how important it is to get out of the building and source from the crowds.

6. *Remix and connect.* At the start of the social media era, fashion led the way in sparking conversations with customers and paying attention to trendsetters. Fashion firms have accepted that the locus of expertise has shifted to the end user and that they'd better pay attention. A great example is the addition of hip-hop and pop culture star Rihanna to the house of LVMH Moët Hennessy Louis Vuitton. She is not a formally trained fashion designer, but she is a style maven, trendsetter, and savvy businesswoman with an inclusive beauty brand, Fenty; 92 million Twitter followers; and 74 million Instagram followers—and counting.

7. *Open-source sharing.* Fashion embraced sourcing from the crowds early on in order to be relevant. Take the graphic design T-shirt company Threadless, founded in 2000. Its genius is that by crowdsourcing graphic concepts for tees from its customers, it masters inventory management by making to order instead of making to stock.

Borrow from fashion thinking and discover that when applied singularly or in combination with each other, these principles can help to creatively disrupt your perspective and identify a new approach or outcome.

USE WHAT YOU HAVE

Don't make excuses about a lack of time, suboptimal staffing, or scarce funding to put off creating. Creativity loves constraints. All that you need is right within you and sitting before your eyes. You must shift your paradigm.

Take, for example, hip-hop music. My generation, Gen X, is responsible for hip-hop music, currently the number one music genre in the world. You're welcome! But let's examine its origins. In the midst of the greatest rollback in funding for arts education in public schools in the late 1970s, black teenagers figured out a new musical instrument: the turntable. As formal teaching in music diminished in public schools, the scratching of the record player's needle on vinyl rose to the level of a percussion instrument. Now that's a paradigm shift! It is that level of reframing and repurposing that continues to spark hip-hop artists such as DJ King Britt, who, while rooted in hip-hop, R&B, and jazz, has acquired an adept muscle for constantly remixing what is in front of him—literally.

Another example comes from Susan Jin Davis, the chief sustainability officer at Comcast. She shared how her cultural identity as a Korean American helped her to develop novel tactics: "As a child of immigrants, there is no blueprint. I've had to be creative to figure out my own path." Susan credits her cultural identity as a marginalized minority with building her capacity to have vision and resilience in building the sustainability practice at Comcast.

To shift your paradigm, start with wonder. Ask, "Why not . . . ?" and "How come . . . ?" You could also start with rigor, by forcing yourself to make do with constraints and stretch them to their limit. Ultimately, just start. Don't make excuses; follow the bread crumbs and see where they lead you.

CREATIVITY LEAP EXERCISE

FOR YOU
► Create a list of wonder mentors and rigor mentors: i.e., creativity mentors! What do you like about them? What about their work speaks to you? What can you borrow from them and put your own spin on?

FOR YOUR ORGANIZATION
► SCAMPER is a mnemonic that stands for *substitute, combine, adapt, modify, put to another use, eliminate, reverse*. It's used in fashion for product development. Try applying two of the principles to jump-start a service, process, or experience that your team is developing.

CHAPTER 9

GET OUT OF THE BUILDING
FINAL THOUGHTS ON INCREASING YOUR CQ

SEE THINGS DIFFERENTLY

You may be aware of the Indian parable about the blind men and the elephant. As each man touched the huge and complex animal, he described it differently. When one touched the tusks, he described the elephant as a smooth and hard-surfaced creature; when another touched its ears, he described it as a soft creature; and when another touched the thick, wrinkly skin around the elephant's ankles, he described the elephant as a rough and coarse animal. The moral of the story is that perspective is everything. But how often do you remember this as you go about working with colleagues and clients pretty much in the same ways you have always done?

Creativity requires diverse perspectives for getting to answers and new insights—and multiple means are required to get those diverse perspectives. I'm not a fan of relying on just one or even two methods like surveys and focus groups to determine what your customer needs. In both of these methods, there is a major gap analysis you must recognize. For surveys, respondents tend to fall along the tails of the bell curve: Those who choose to respond either are overjoyed and in love with your service or product, or despise it for a range of reasons that the survey won't necessarily yield. The latter group is out for blood. The challenge with focus groups is that once people who do not know and trust each other are sequestered away in a room, they predictably fall into sheep mode. That is to say, they don't want to rock the boat and share what they *really* think. The extroverts and bossy pants in the room tend to sway the direction of the conversation.

Both of these methods showcase the difference between what people say and what they do. For example, let's say I am asked on a survey or in a focus group, "How often do you exercise?" I might fib a bit and respond "Oh, five days a week," when in fact I am lucky if I get around to exercising two days a week. This is where alternative qualitative research methods such as interviews, observation, and contextual inquiry come in handy. In order to understand the nuanced drivers for my gym attendance, you may learn a lot more by observing my behaviors rather than what I self-report. My attendance may have less to do with the location of the gym or price point of the gym membership and more to do with childcare issues or public transportation challenges.

The best methodology is not binary, but rather a hybrid approach, which integrates both quantitative and qualitative research methods. Quantitative research shows us the bird's-eye view and aggregated patterns of behavior. It shows us the "what." Qualitative research shows us the worm's-eye view, the "why" factors that are driving people's behaviors. When used in complementary ways, qualitative and quantitative research can put the meat on the bones of the story you are creating.

Dancers and musicians are experts at learning how to see in different ways. For example, when dancers learn choreography, they are mastering pattern recognition. They learn how to see movement outside of their body, incorporate it into their own, and execute it into motion that delivers meaning and story. Music theory, feeling rhythm, and identifying the relationships between notes is a different form of pattern recognition that gets heightened for musicians.

When we understand dancers' work process in particular, there are huge lessons to apply to our own work. Tinkering and moving in order to make and discover can spur us on to try prototyping, developing our work in iterative stages, and getting more physical with our work. In the 2019 Steelcase report "New Work. New Rules," Donna Flynn, the vice president of Work-Space Futures at Steelcase, said, "Our brains and bodies need to move to be creative."[1] The body activates the brain to make ideas even better. Physical movement affects how we think.

A second way to practice the lessons from dancers is to get out of our offices and visit our customers on their own terms and in their own context. That movement will go miles in helping you see things from a new angle. Do not be surprised if shifting your work habits in this way compels you to revise your original plan, start over, or add in entirely new ideas, people, or direction to the mix. While this may be uncomfortable at first, it is all part of the process that is required to take our gnarly, tangled ball of yarns (our challenges), unravel them, and stretch them out to their simplest glory.

As head of Venture Lab at ZX Ventures, the global growth and innovation group within AB InBev, Mirko Lagattolla regularly makes sure that his team gets out of the building to see things differently. His team is responsible for identifying what's next in beverages from a customer-centric perspective. To do so, he told me,

you have to force yourself to go into the street, go into
the bar, and observe a person walking up to the bar,
ordering, waiting, getting the beverage, paying, talking
to people, etc. We look at the overall experience and
come up with ideas about how we can improve the
experience. Next we test our ideas as in a true lab.

This type of kinesthetic discovery is what Mirko has grown
to appreciate. He admits that 10 years ago he had a very different mind-set:

I thought that everything could be engineered and
planned. But along the way, I learned that creativity is
really the foil of everything we do in our life. If we don't
have creativity, we will stop evolving as human beings.

Mirko also indicated that it takes a bit of courage and
brazenness to work in this more direct way, integrated into
the customer's environment. Getting out of the building is a
creativity leap. Until we shift our perspective, we can't possibly
know what we don't know.

BE A TRANSLATOR

Researching what people really need and want requires acts
of translation. In fact, translation is one of the most common
creativity leaps we perform daily in our work. Whenever you
explain what it is you do to a different team or department in
your company, you are engaging in an act of translation. You
must shift gears to determine the best way to communicate
what your work entails. You are traversing from one domain
to another to figure out how to represent what you do in a
coherent way. That is a creative act. This is why Jeff Benjamin,
COO of the Vetri restaurant group and Fitler Club in Philadelphia, thinks of communication as his canvas and his artistic medium. When you are required to translate the way you

approach your work, you are forced to disrupt yourself—that's what happened to Adam Karasick.

Adam is the senior manager for enterprise technology at EisnerAmper, a global accounting and advisory firm. He arrived at EisnerAmper as a CPA who also had the practical experience of working in a financial software firm. The data modeling work he was exposed to at the software firm helped him understand how to apply that skill set for business transformation.

Jeff Buchakjian is a partner and forensic accounting expert at the same firm. Jeff happened to be one of the first people Adam reached out to as he was pivoting in his career and making cold calls to forensic accounting firms. Jeff is well aware that the accounting field is getting disrupted by technology and wants to ensure that EisnerAmper is at the forefront of anticipating changes. That is why he made an investment in Adam: "Once Adam was already here as an accountant and showed a genuine interest in, and personal experience with, software and technology—we decided to pay for him to get his master's in data analytics."

As the bridge between technical accounting and computer science at EisnerAmper, Adam's primary role is translation. He explained:

> My work process? I try to think from the perspective of my audience. A lot of the programs I work on require advanced data modeling. [For example,] how to make my accounts payable system talk to my revenue system and to procurement—all of which may be on different platforms. I don't necessarily need to do the technical talk. I just need to show that "this may be the result if we take a specific path." My goal is to get the necessary buy-in, and I do so by speaking the necessary language.

Your translation skills are key to creativity: translation is how you get buy-in; buy-in is key to collaboration; and collaboration yields the most dynamic creative results. Acts of translation aren't always verbal. Translating complex ideas into visual story form (doodles work well) often is the best way for your intended audience to understand your value proposition. This is because our brains are designed for us to be innately visual. The fight-flight-freeze trigger rooted in our hypothalamus has enabled us to survive by reading the visual landscape in seconds.

Bob Schwartz, vice president of global design and user experience at GE Healthcare, has learned that trust and relationship building are also key to getting the buy-in that yields creative results. He credits that realization in part to a stint in his career when he worked at Procter & Gamble. Upon arrival, his boss, Claudia Kotchka, considered an early apostle of design thinking in the USA, told him to "Go learn!" And with that directive, he did a series of two-week rotations throughout the various design departments. One of the things he learned was that all good teaming begins and ends with relationships:

> Create a safe environment where people feel they can express their true selves. You know the name of their spouse, when their birthday is. If you don't build relationships, people won't trust you, and they won't want to work with you.

In his career, Bob has become very good at creating coalitions of disparate people, and he has three guiding principles: First, to be subversive with goodness in your heart. Second, to make it about everyone else. And third, to recruit the army you do not control:

> The bridge that allows the connection between empathy and curiosity is to show up as a businessperson

and meet leaders where they are. Help them solve their problems by using the empathic and curious approaches to learn about design and business—then they will tell your story for you.

Translation is about creating meaning out of disparate bits of information. In that sense, it is not unlike bricolage, the French art of making use of whatever is at hand. Social anthropologist Claude Lévi-Strauss wrote about bricolage in his 1966 work *The Savage Mind*. He likened bricolage to a junk man putting together a new tractor from random parts at his disposal.

Bricolage is a characteristic of organizational improvising. The bricoleur is the resourceful person who pulls together discarded bits and pieces of material and information to make new and fresh solutions. The improvising bricoleur engages in careful translation—from junk to useful object—using wonder and rigor, observation and intuition.

We see bricolage when teams spontaneously reconstruct events in order to make meaning and create order from chaos. This is what happened when the creative team at VaynerMedia worked with Budweiser to promote their brand based on a pivotal moment in NBA star Dwyane Wade's career.

Adam Lock is the group creative director at VaynerMedia who led the team that produced an award-winning social video for Budweiser featuring Wade. The NBA player is known for swapping his jersey with other basketball legends. Adam and his team were tasked with finding a way to make a connection between Budweiser as a purpose-driven brand and Wade, who had transcended what was on the court. They did this by shifting him from the hero archetype to the caregiver archetype. In an emotional display, Wade was presented with shirts, jackets, and gowns from carefully selected people whose lives he had touched. The process of developing such a viral video is most relevant here.

Adam described how up until the final edit they had no idea what the emotional impact of the video would be. The team tends to start very broadly and ideates hundreds of concepts. They brought in colleagues from a range of departments across the company. They decided to create the entire video without a script because they believed there was a story to tell through the sport of basketball itself. The entire process took six weeks— from the time they sold the idea to Budweiser to the moment it was posted on social media. This was an aggressive timeline. The messy part started when they tried to go from idea to execution. "We were working with real people, and real stories, and only had three hours with Wade to capture as much as possible. And without a script."

It turned out that using time as a pressure cooker was ultimately helpful. It forced them to make decisions and focus on key elements. "We didn't have the luxury of time, and in reality, that was the right way to approach it," Adam explained. The process that his team uses for collecting insights included social listening. Vayner community managers sat around sifting through Instagram, Twitter, and Facebook to observe what a range of people were talking about in their daily lives. Insight gathering also came from their colleagues on the strategy teams. Adam said that the "quality of a really great insight is like a semiprecious rock. You always have your ears listening and ready to hear something that could be a game changer." Intuition is key here because there are no textbook solutions. Making decisions based on a combination of knowledge, experience, and confidence and asking "Does this feel right?" is key to his process.

Improvisation was also critical in executing the final video, an unscripted piece. Adam shared that trust was an important ingredient in the process. Without having multiple rounds to check things, it took lots of confidence that in the moment, the team would pull it off. That included the casting directors who interviewed and selected strangers to share their compelling and personal stories about Wade's impact.

Ultimately, the Dwyane Wade Budweiser video won three Cannes Film Festival awards, the agency's first. Adam had two takeaways from the process. The first was the importance of timing and the power of a great idea at a great time.

> Clients are looking for ways to drive attention—they want to send shock waves through Twitter. . . . So launching this commercial the morning of the day of Wade's last home game meant that it was picked up and we gave everyone something other than Wade's career to talk about.

The second takeaway was the importance of authenticity. While the creative team may want to claim ownership for being the originator of the idea, Adam said that this whole concept came from Wade. What Adam's team can be credited for is finding a powerful way to translate Wade's story to video.

Adam's work process demonstrates that stories are data too. Like the bricoleur, we must be able to look at and reimagine what is, in order to discern what is coming next. One way to do that is to complement quantitative big data with qualitative data: stories.

In 2012, my dad was very sick, dying of stage 4 non-Hodgkin lymphoma. During his multiple stays at various hospitals, we often felt like we were futilely chasing the disease: one step forward and two steps back. His suffering would change overnight, or even from one hour to the next. My mom, my sister, and I quickly learned that the nurses were often the most insightful, consistent, and reliable source of updates about our dad. One afternoon during a visit, my dad nodded off to sleep and I wandered into the hallway to stretch my legs. I saw a man in a white physician's coat walking briskly toward my father's room. He stopped in a doorway just before the room and started asking a nurse a series of questions. I overheard him say "Mr. Weathers," and, recognizing my dad's name, I ventured over to him.

I introduced myself as Mr. Weathers's daughter and asked if he was inquiring about my dad. He brusquely replied that he was, and that he was one of the specialists. When I learned what he was asking about, I began to share what the last nurse on duty had told me. The specialist interrupted me and said that he would wait for the rest of the graphs and charts to come in. I was affronted by how coldly he stopped my explanation. I decided to tell him that there was information beyond the numbers, charts, and graphs that could help him understand how my father was doing. "Stories are data too," I told him. He apologized and listened half-heartedly to the rest of what I had to say.

I share my experience because it demonstrates what happens when we have a myopic view about what counts as data: We risk missing the bigger picture, losing out on empathy, and ignoring opportunities to collaborate with a broader segment of our network to solve problems.

PLAY

Geraldine Laybourne proclaimed to me, "Children are wonder and inspiration." She would know. As the founder of children's cable network Nickelodeon, she is a legendary media maven. And while children at play became her business to know, she also found ways to integrate those lessons into the design of the workday:

> We started with 20 people. As we became more successful, everyone wanted to be in every meeting. When we had 400 employees, meetings were wall to wall. I decided that every day at 3:00 there would be no meetings: Recess! Maybe we did it for about six months— but it sent a message.

It didn't matter that the recess phenomenon lasted for only six months. The point is that Gerry exercised an experimental mind-set to prototype a new activity. It set the tone for the ways that Gerry would introduce play in other aspects of work, such as meetings.

> I really believe in meetings that are show-and-tell in a creative way. So, every six to eight weeks we had an all-hands meeting, and someone who had made something cool would present it. This was stuff people had created, and we were letting them have the sunlight and the credit. It wasn't reports. It was pure fun! There were refreshments and people bonded.
>
> When it felt to me like we were getting too comfortable with pitches from outside producers, we started an experimental creative lab. People didn't have to have a finite product.

Those "pure fun" moments are important to keep alive in our organizations. That is because "when we play, the brain is learning how to learn." This statement from neuroscientist Bill Klem really stuck with me as I listened to him on an episode of the podcast *The Pulse* titled "Why We Play."[2] It underscored for me how tightly intertwined play is with creativity. Play taps into multiple dimensions of our creative existence on the levels of mind, body, and community. It is essential for any creative endeavor.

Play is also part of our evolutionary path. In the "Why We Play" podcast episode, Kathy Hirsh-Pasek, a professor of psychology at Temple University described it as "a vehicle for achieving powerful learning." Mentally, play contributes to brain health because it strengthens our ability to switch back and forth between the frontal cortex and limbic region of the brain. It also allows us to experience some mental relaxation, to take a break from work's emphasis on the frontal cortex. Play is rooted in the moment, and so it has the capacity to help us transcend whatever ails us. It lightens our moods and increases optimism; it makes us more open to making new connections and seeking out new experiences.

Physically, the active elements of play revive us. Getting out of our brain and into our body ultimately creates new neural pathways. Whether we are jumping up and down during a card game of Uno, playacting through a game of charades, or running around outside while we toss a ball back and forth, the kinesthetic nature of play is a recharge. It releases happy hormones like serotonin and endorphins. It reduces stress, calms us, and primes us for the wonder and rigor of creativity. Play is as important to our brain and physical health as sleep.

What if your work could become your play? Gary Chick, a play researcher, proclaimed on the same episode of *The Pulse* that he gets a kick out of doing research. "That's my play. Doing statistics and computer programming—I like that."

It is a bit strange that we have become accustomed to dividing up time between work and play. Play is not embedded into the way we work beyond the occasional memes of foosball and ping-pong tables strategically positioned in the cool kids' companies. Why the boundary? It goes back to how we have been educated, in blocks and chunks of time separating moments of learning in the classroom from moments of playfulness in the schoolyard. But as Mr. Rogers said, "Play gives children a chance to practice what they are learning."[3] Rogers, the famous TV personality who had many a preschooler (myself included) glued daily to the television, understood that it is a false dichotomy to separate play from learning.

We don't play enough in American society. One day, anthropologists and historians may look back on this lack of play as an epidemic, one that meant we attained only a fraction of the amount of innovation that was actually possible. If, as psychologist Abraham Maslow is said to have asserted, "almost all creativity involves purposeful play," then we need to get on with it, especially in our pursuit of innovation.

The net result of our beliefs about play is that we treat vacationing and leisure like guilty pleasures instead of as sacred pauses. We differ greatly in this sense from most of our European, Asian, Latin American, and African friends and colleagues—that is to say, from the rest of the world. When I worked in global fashion sourcing, producing bras and panties for the Victoria's Secret brand, our manufacturing partners spanned the globe. Our Italian colleagues unapologetically shut down their offices to vacation for the entire month of August. When I lived in Colombo, Sri Lanka, it was not unusual for a factory to go missing in action when a young woman employed there got married. Her wedding meant a celebration that lasted at least one week and involved extended family, many of whom worked in the factory. Some of us mumbled under our breath in a resentful way as production slowed down. Others of us looked blissfully on at the celebrating employees' resolve and commitment to rest, celebrate, and spend time with their families and friends.

One of the great tragedies in all of the budget cuts for public school education in the United States is the phasing out of gym and art classes where children are free to play. Jack Ma, founder of Chinese e-commerce giant Alibaba, has spoken publicly about his belief that in school, children should be less focused on science and more on learning how to play. Treating physical movement and artistic exploration as secondary to "real" subjects like mathematics, science, history, and literature is a tragic miss. Our learning environments tend to be very structured and orderly: the places where we learn to stay in line. And then we graduate people from that environment into more boxes: the corporate environment of sitting in office cubicles. We ask people to think outside the box while expecting them to literally work in boxes.

Play is wonder and rigor to the max. It is during play that children are self-motivated to ponder big questions, to improvise, and to follow their hearts—to be creative and to innovate. This is why I was so encouraged when I learned about Double Dutch Dreamz, based in Harlem, New York. Founded by 70-year-old Malika Whitney, Double Dutch Dreamz continues the legacy of jumping rope as a way for kids to build confidence, learn performance, improvise, and collaborate. As one little girl said, "I feel bravery when I jump into the rope." Malika has even taken Double Dutch to the blind community.

So many public schools in American cities have asphalt playgrounds. In fact, many of the playgrounds double as the teachers' parking lot. Given what we know about play's benefits, what might this do over time to an entire segment of our society? What might be the long-term cost to innovation in our society? Sharon Danks, an environmental planner, has become an advocate for green schoolyards through the program Green Schoolyards America because, as she puts it, schoolyards are "our most well-used public parkland, completely undeveloped."[4]

The success of the Burning Man festival is a symptom of our human need to play and practice wonder. Cofounded in 1986 by Larry Harvey and Jerry James, Burning Man is a self-organizing, adaptive, and emergent (sound familiar?) festival in the Black Rock Desert in Nevada. It is grounded in 10 core principles: inclusion, gifting, decommodification, self-reliance, self-expression, communal effort, civic responsibility, leave no trace, participation, and immediacy.

Manager Maryann Hulsman said in a public radio interview on August 15, 2019, that Burning Man is "an opportunity to practice radical creativity in the desert."[5] The growth in popularity of the Burning Man festival indicates people's need to break away from the stresses of a daily grind through play. By dressing up, imagining new ways of being, and experimenting in new environments, attendees (aka "burners") find the wonder and purpose we all sorely need.

Like the Burning Man burners, we need to get messy and wild and take breaks from the routine. This is how we begin to integrate creativity into our work processes. Play is a fantastic and accessible place to start.

LEAP!

Increasing your creativity quotient is about building on what has come before you. And that requires, well, building. Building is ambiguous and messy. While we may start with a plan, plans shift, agendas change, and assumptions are challenged. Creativity's ROI is a return on inquiry, on improvisation, and on intuition. These returns can be scaled to benefit you personally as well as organizationally. There are three leaps I encourage you to make regularly in order to optimize your creativity ROI.

Leap from Prioritizing Deep Specialization to Valuing Broad Experience

When's the last time you got out of the office? I mean really got out of the office in order to spark wonder? New experiences and environments are important to expand the boundaries of your work. Do not be confined to your sector, geographic location, or usual coterie of experts to get insights and advice.

Leap from Deferring Only to What's Rational to Embracing Ambiguity

In complex systems, answers and solutions are not immediately obvious. They emerge over time, like a shadowy figure from the fog at dusk. Murky and ambiguous contexts require the rigor to sit with ambiguity until a recognizable picture begins to emerge; they insist that you play the long game in order to get to understanding and insight. In practice, that could mean switching up whom you have logically identified as the expert in the organization (think about it: that frontline salesperson may not have the status and perspective of an executive vice president, but she sure is privy to conversations, questions, and comments that illuminate what is going well and what is going poorly in your offering).

Leap from Organizational Silos to Networked Community

Depicting our organizations with boxes and arrows and developing linear processes for product launches have one thing in common: they give us a false sense of security. In reality, our org charts are more like messy mind maps, and our products, services, and experiences exist in a macro-environment full of ambiguity and uncertainty that eschews linear thinking.

The best way to rebound from a situation that catches you off guard is to have fluid structures in place. Try taking away some of the structure and leaving space for more open inquiry, improvisation, and intuition. Keep in mind that markets are unpredictable and inconsistent because they are made up of people. Embrace it.

These three leaps show that creativity can be best navigated when you broaden your perspective and your inputs. Move, translate, and play to challenge your assumptions and navigate complex situations. This is how you increase your creative competency. This is how you make the creativity leap.

CREATIVITY LEAP EXERCISE

FOR YOU

► The word *dérive* is French for "drift." It's a great way to describe, for example, the wandering that naturally happens as you walk through the serpentine streets of Venice, Italy. Go get lost on purpose during your lunch break, or drive a different way to or from work without the aid of a GPS. Notice how you feel and what you discover.

FOR YOUR ORGANIZATION

► Require your employees to annually attend a conference completely unrelated to your sector or industry. Ask them to share with the team what they learned and whom they met. Then determine what could be applied to your own work.

APPENDIX

21 QUESTIONS AND SUGGESTIONS TO JUMP-START YOUR CREATIVITY

Use these questions as prompts for personal journaling or to start a team discussion.

1. What new hobby can you start outside of work?

2. What is an example of something you are doing where you are a complete beginner? How does it feel? What elements from that experience could you bring to your work?

3. What do you like to play? What do you think that says about you?

4. How often do you daydream?

5. When was the last time you got lost? What happened? How did you deal with getting lost?

6. When was the last time you went off-script and improvised? How did it feel?

7. When was the last time you listened to your gut and followed your intuition? What was the result? What did you learn from that experience?

8. Are you comfortable with ambiguity? Share an example.

9. Do the following short experiment: Keep track of how often you ask questions during the workday with your colleagues. What sorts of questions do they tend to be?

10. If you found yourself with a free afternoon, what would you ideally want to do with that found time?

11. What would an audit of the physical environment of your work office yield? What would it demonstrate and show?

12. Write a postmortem of your work projects. What does it say about you? Where is there an opportunity to add in more creativity?

13. Can you attend at least one conference or gathering a year that is outside of your industry or comfort zone? Try it and share your insights with colleagues.

14. Does your company hire from the same sources, countries, or universities? Why? What might happen if they mixed that up?

15. Do you rotate who leads meetings? Start experimenting with this once a quarter.

16. Are there divergent areas for relaxation and zoning out in your workplace?

17. How often do you host meetings outdoors or while walking? Try hosting your next two meetings outdoors or while walking.

18. What if you tried explaining an idea only with doodles? Try it and collect feedback.

19. Purchase a magazine from a field you have utterly no interest in. Browse through it and identify at least three approaches or ideas that could be metaphors useful for your work.

20. What are your mentor brands? Think of companies, brands, or experiences that are outside of your own industry but inspire and engage you. In other words, who do you want to be when you grow up, professionally?

21. At what would you consider yourself an expert? This could be playing golf, dancing salsa, doing dishes under five minutes, or planning a road trip. What did it take for you to develop that expertise? What elements could you bring forward into your work?

WONDERRIGOR GAME

I created the WonderRigor™ Discovery Deck, a game to help practice the ideas in this book.[1] Think of it as a creativity tool for business. These cards take you through three phases: Mindset, Mode, and Catalyst. Phase 1: prime your mind and those of your teammates with Mindset cards. Phase 2: work through an actual challenge by choosing a future-state Mode card. Phase 3: identify a way to keep the momentum going through a Catalyst card.

The Mindset cards get you out of your typical way of thinking. For example, you may pull a card explaining the Japanese philosophy of *wabi-sabi*, which is about the acceptance of transience and imperfection. The prompt would ask you, "How comfortable are you with ambiguity? Share a time when you felt great uncertainty and flowed with it. Why did you take that approach, and what have you learned from it?" In Phase 2, you must first identify a challenge or project that you and your team are working through.

Familiarize yourself with the four different modes/modalities of WonderRigor: Specialize, Hack, Provoke, and Invent (see Figure 4). These are all along a WonderRigor continuum. The idea is to never be stagnant but rather to identify which mode is necessary depending on the challenge at hand. Specialize is when you value details, repetitive practice, proven results, and deep expertise. Hack is when you value expediency over quality in order to discover new things quickly. Select Provoke when you want to cause others to think and act in ways beyond the constraints of the present and consider what might be. And choose Invent when you have spent equal time in the trenches as well as allowed yourself to do big blue-sky thinking in order to become a market leader.

It is important to remember that the goal is not to always remain in one mode. These modes are not archetypes. Rather,

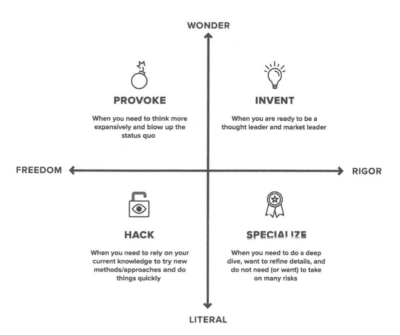

Figure 4. The four modes of wonder and rigor.

they are lenses that you should try on. They will help you to identify new ways of working through your selected challenge. Pick a mode that you want to try on in the future state, working through a problem. The Mode cards help you simulate various levels of diverging and converging through a project and problem-solving. So, for example, if you've been doing a lot of brainstorming up until the present state, then try on the mode of Specialize. The card prompts in this category would help you and your team identify where and how to bring deep expertise, skill, and rigor into the process.

Goals are dreams with deadlines. And that's what the Catalyst cards help with in the final phase. They help you to identify tactics. You'll be prompted to assign short-term, mid-term, and long-term goals to achieve the desired future state.

Setting these goals makes it more likely that you will do so. For example, the Catalyst cards may require you to identify a figure (or organization) that exhibits wonder and then prompt you to contact them within the next month and have a conversation about how they specifically practice wonder. Or you may pull a card that requires you to write down a plan of how you will commit to more rigor in your work over the next seven days.

Enjoy the creativity leaps that these prompts spark!

GLOSSARY

chaord: A term coined by Dee Hock; it is a helpful way to understand complexity. Chaords are systems consisting of both chaos (or randomness) and order (or structure).

complexity: Any adaptive, self-organizing, and emergent system. Examples are creativity, jazz, and improvisation. Since creativity is a complex system, I recommend that we navigate the complexity in our world with complexity—i.e., creativity. It's a similar principle to removing chewing gum from the bottom of your shoe with chewing gum.

creativity: A person's ability to toggle between wonder and rigor in order to solve problems and produce novel value. Creativity is a competency and is the engine for innovation.

gap: A distance or divide between a present state and a future state. Currently there is a skills gap, and people need help adapting to ubiquitous technology where tasks are increasingly done by robots or artificial intelligence. People will need skills in complex problem-solving, creating the algorithms for the technology, interpersonal skills, envisioning, and strategy work.

innovation: Invention converted into value. Creativity is the engine.

leap: Generating energy to bridge a gap, a divide, or a chasm. There is currently a skills gap for the fourth industrial revolution (4IR), where technology is ubiquitous. Applying creativity's

3 I's (inquiry, improvisation, and intuition) is the way to make the leap and bridge that gap.

rigor: A person's capacity to exercise deep skill, attention to detail, discipline, and time on task for mastery.

the 3 I's: The 3 I's—inquiry, improvisation, and intuition—are tactics to produce creativity. They are the means to the end.

1. **Inquiry.** The root of wisdom and the precursor to empathy. It requires an information gap and an ability to frame and reframe questions. Asking questions is a way of thinking.

2. **Improvisation.** Building on ideas within minimal constraints. Improvisation is not doing whatever you feel like; it has rules, fluid structures, that help you to embrace mistakes, be deeply observant, and be adaptive. Examples of great improvisation are in jazz, rap, comedy, excellent sales/customer service experiences, and scientific experimentation.

3. **Intuition.** Visceral, internal wisdom that produces pattern recognition and insight for decision-making. Harriet Tubman, Albert Einstein, and Steve Jobs are examples of famous innovators and leaders who relied on and valued their intuition coupled with their rational intellect to make decisions.

wonder: A person's capacity to exercise awe, pausing, dreaming, and audacious blue-sky thinking.

NOTES

Chapter 1—Create Like Your Life Depends on It

1. Dider Bonnet, Jerome Buvat, and Subrahmanyam KVJ, "When Digital Disruption Strikes: How Can Incumbents Respond?" *Digital Transformation Review*, no. 7 (February 2015): 78–90.
2. Ben Gilbert, "A group of major US companies just took out a full-page NYT ad pushing Apple, Amazon, and Walmart to 'get to work' prioritizing social responsibility over profits," *Business Insider*, August 26, 2019, https://www.businessinsider.com/amazon-apple-walmart-nyt-ad-ben-jerrys-patagonia-social-responsibility-2019-8.
3. Steelcase, "New Work. New Rules," *360° Exploring Innovation at Work*, issue 75 (2019), https://www.steelcase.com/research/360-magazine/new-work-new-rules.
4. "Laura Linney on What Makes Good Criticism," *Hello Monday with Jessi Hempel*, October 21, 2019, http://hellomondaywithjessihempel.libsyn.com/laura-linney-on-what -makes-good-criticism-0.
5. Warren Berger, *A More Beautiful Question: The Power of Inquiry to Spark Breakthrough Ideas* (New York: Bloomsbury USA, 2016).

Chapter 3—Inquire: Ask a Better Friggin' Question

1. M. Tamra Chandler, *Feedback (and Other Dirty Words): Why We Fear It, How to Fix It* (Oakland, CA: Berrett-Koehler Publishers, 2019).
2. Natalie Kitroeff and David Gelles, "Claims of Shoddy Production Draw Scrutiny to a Second Boeing Jet," *New York Times*, April 20, 2019, https://www.nytimes.com/2019/04/20/business/boeing-dreamliner-production-problems.html.
3. Andrew Ross Sorkin interview with Ray Dalio at the *New York Times* DealBook conference, December 11, 2014, https://www.youtube.com/watch?v=v812IV-NFFY.

4. Sorkin and Dalio interview, *New York Times* DealBook conference.
5. Ian Leslie, *Curious: The Desire to Know and Why Your Future Depends on It* (New York: Basic Books, 2014).

Chapter 4—Improvise: Leverage Organized Chaos

1. Frank J. Barrett, *Yes to the Mess: Surprising Leadership Lessons from Jazz* (Boston: Harvard Business Review Press, 2012).
2. Dee Hock, *One from Many: VISA and the Rise of Chaordic Organization* (San Francisco: Berrett-Koehler Publishers, 2005).
3. Steelcase, "New Work. New Rules."

Chapter 5—Intuit: Put Bravery before Mastery

1. Sophy Birnbaum, *The Art of Intuition: Cultivating Your Inner Wisdom* (New York: Jeremy P. Tarcher, 2011).
2. William Duggan, *Strategic Intuition: The Creative Spark in Human Achievement* (New York: Columbia University Press, 2007).
3. Walter Isaacson, *Steve Jobs* (New York: Simon & Schuster, 2011), 48.

Chapter 6—Commune: Come Together to Create

1. Seth Godin, *Tribes: We Need You to Lead Us* (New York: Portfolio, 2008).
2. The *Line of Sight* installation was designed by JPL visual strategist Lois Kim.

Chapter 7—Forecast: Amplify What Is Uniquely Human

1. Galit Ariel, "From killer robots to automated colleagues," *Futur•ithmic*, July 9, 2019, https://www.futurithmic.com/2019/07/09/from-killer-robots-to-automated-colleagues/.
2. "Balder Onarheim: Training Your Brain to Do the Impossible," EmTech France 2017, YouTube, March 1, 2018, https://www.youtube.com/watch?v=WetsMpkRgBw.
3. Deborah Bothun and Art Kleiner, "The Next Pop Superstar Just Might Be a Robot," *strategy+business*, issue 87 (Summer 2017), https://www.strategy-business.com/article/The-Next-Pop-Superstar-Just-Might-Be-a-Robot?gko=f254d.

Chapter 8—Remix, Reframe, Repurpose

1. Austin Kleon, *Steal Like an Artist: 10 Things Nobody Told You About Being Creative* (New York: Workman Publishing, 2012).

2. Margaret Mark and Carol S. Pearson, *The Hero and the Outlaw: Building Extraordinary Brands Through the Power of Archetypes* (New York: McGraw-Hill, 2001).
3. Johanna Blakley, "Lessons from Fashion's Free Culture," TEDxUSC, April 2010, https://www.ted.com/talks/johanna_blakley_lessons_from_fashion_s_free_culture?language=en.
4. Natalie W. Nixon and Johanna Blakley, "Fashion Thinking: Towards an Actionable Methodology," *Fashion Practice* 4, issue 2 (2012): 153–75, DOI:10.2752/175693812X13403765252262.

Chapter 9—Get Out of the Building: Final Thoughts on Increasing Your CQ

1. Steelcase, "New Work. New Rules."
2. "Why We Play," *The Pulse*, WHYY/PBS, accessed August 16, 2019, https://whyy.org/episodes/why-we-play/.
3. Sara Dewitt, "How PBS Kids Puts Play at the Center of Digital Content Development," Fred Rogers Center, December 10, 2013, https://www.fredrogerscenter.org/2013/12/how-pbs-kids-puts-play-at-the-center-of-digital-content-development/.
4. Nina Feldman, "Why your neighborhood school probably doesn't have a playground," *Radio Times*, WHYY, February 6, 2019, https://whyy.org/articles/uneven-play-most-philadelphia-public-schools-dont-have-playgrounds-thats-slowly-changing/.
5. "Sick Burn: The Future of Free Expression at Burning Man," *1A*, WAMU 88.5, August 15, 2019, https://thela.org/shows/2019-08-15/sick-burn-the-future-of-free-expression-at-burning-man.

Appendix

1. For more information, see http://www.figure8thinking.com. The WonderRigor Discovery Deck is available on Amazon.

ACKNOWLEDGMENTS

This book has marinated for a good five years. I appreciate all of the audiences and workshop participants who experienced variations of the WonderRigor Discovery Deck prototypes. That includes folks at d.school Paris, IBM Design, Steelcase, Pennovation, O3 World, CENTRO, Business Innovation Factory, CUSP, BigSpeak audiences, Bloomberg, and a convening by Mickey Munley of university development officers. Your feedback at every turn was invaluable.

The writing process takes a village. I am super-grateful to Joseph Pine, coauthor of *The Experience Economy*, for forwarding along my book proposal to the team at Berrett-Koehler. Were it not for his introductory email, this book's production would have turned out quite differently. Thank you to my editor Neal Maillet at Berrett-Koehler for taking a chance on seeing to it that my ideas about creativity got into book form. Much respect to Danielle Goodman, my developmental editor, for all of her thoughtful and carefully crafted questions and suggestions. She's a gem. And my gratitude goes to the entire team at Berrett-Koehler for their thorough attention to detail for the book's launch.

Editing is a painful, necessary, and magical part of writing. And there is a lot left on the cutting-room floor. Many people gave their time, thoughts, and energy to be interviewed for this book, but not every great quote or anecdote made it into this final version. I am grateful to all of the business professionals who graciously took time out of their busy lives to allow me to interview them about how creativity shows up in their practice: Galit Ariel of WondARlands; Celine Barel of International Flavors and Fragrances; Ben Batory of Franklin Templeton Investments; Kevin Bethune of dreams • design + life; Kelley Black of Balancing the Executive Life; King Britt, international DJ and music producer; Jeff Buchakjian and Adam Karasick of Eisner-Amper; Jim Caruso of Simplura; Kelley Case, Dan Goods, and Brent Sherwood of NASA's Jet Propulsion Lab; Norris Childs and Randy Frederick of the Philadelphia Beekeepers Guild; Christine Cox, artistic and executive director of BalletX; Len Damico and James Koran of Arcweb Technologies; Susan Jin Davis and Karima Zedan of Comcast; Maaike Doyer of Business Models Inc.; Nima Etemadi and Lily Fischer of Cake Life Bake Shop; Dag Folger and Peter Knutson of A+I; Sean Forman of Sports Reference; Michael Forman of FS Investments; Nancy Frost of Bank of the West; Daphne Goldberg, MD; David Gutstadt, Jeff Benjamin, and Amanda Potter of Fitler Club; John Harker of Harker Plumbing; Julian Harzheim; Anne Hogan of the University of Memphis; Ira Kalish of Deloitte; Melanie King; Melissa Koujakian of République; Ari Kushner of Accenture; Mirko Lagattolla of AB InBev; Geraldine Laybourne; Genein Letford; Mart Maasik of SEB Bank; John Maeda, EVP chief experience officer at Publicis Sapient; Vivek Mahapatra of Salesforce; Gary and Amy Manoff of Manoff Market Gardens and Cidery; Tamera Maresh-Carver of FedEx Express; John Morley of Hitachi Vantara; Safiya Noble of UCLA; Balder Onarheim of PlatoScience; Nicole Pittman of Just Beginnings Collaborative; Dain Saint, musician and game designer; Biplab Sarkar of Vectorworks; Bob Schwartz of GE Healthcare; Bhushan Sethi and John Jones of Pricewaterhouse-Coopers; Carla Silver of Leadership+Design; Claude Silver and Adam Lock of VaynerMedia; Dave Silver, William Toms, and

Ryan Eppley of REC Philly; Daniel Stern, chef and founder of R2L; Randy Swearer of Autodesk; Tina Tweedy of Chocolat Abeille; Matt Vander Laan of MonoSol; Heidi Zak and Ra'el Cohen of ThirdLove; and Paul Zak of Immersion Neuroscience.

Others shared their professional generosity in equally helpful ways. Thanks to Jenn Richey Nicholas and Andrew Nicholas for leading the best graphic and web design company in Philadelphia: Pixel Parlor. Were it not for Pixel Parlor's visualization brilliance, I never would have been able to effectively tell the story of wonder and rigor through images. Valerie Jacobs, Sarah Brooks, Dan Roam, Drew Marshall, Suzi Hamill, and Adrienne Kenton: Thank you for the multiple conversations full of encouragement and feedback. They were vital.

The root and sustenance of my own creativity is my family. As reflected in bits and pieces in the book, my parents, Fred and Carole Weathers, seeded in me a creative confidence. My husband, John Nixon, is my best friend and helped me to remain buoyant: thank you for your love and grace.

INDEX

C

ABOUT THE AUTHOR

© Sahar Coston-Hardy

Author, global speaker, and consultant, Natalie Nixon is a creativity strategist who happily integrates wonder and rigor into her life and work. She converted a 16-year career as a professor into a successful consulting practice. At Figure 8 Thinking, she emboldens leaders to apply creativity and foresight for transformative business results.

Natalie incorporates her background in anthropology and fashion, as well as her experiences living in Brazil, Israel, Germany, Sri Lanka, and Portugal. She's the editor of *Strategic Design Thinking: Innovation in Products, Services, Experiences, and Beyond* and a regular contributor to *Inc.* magazine. Natalie earned a BA (honors) in Anthropology and Africana Studies from Vassar College, an MS in Global Textile Marketing from Thomas Jefferson University, and a PhD in Design Management from the University of Westminster in London.

When she's not dancing up a storm in hip-hop class, she's fine-tuning her foxtrot, salsa, and tango on the ballroom floor. She lives in her hometown of Philadelphia, Pennsylvania, with her husband, John Nixon, and is the proud stepmother of Sydney.

Berrett–Koehler
Publishers

Berrett-Koehler is an independent publisher dedicated to an ambitious mission: *Connecting people and ideas to create a world that works for all.*

Our publications span many formats, including print, digital, audio, and video. We also offer online resources, training, and gatherings. And we will continue expanding our products and services to advance our mission.

We believe that the solutions to the world's problems will come from all of us, working at all levels: in our society, in our organizations, and in our own lives. Our publications and resources offer pathways to creating a more just, equitable, and sustainable society. They help people make their organizations more humane, democratic, diverse, and effective (and we don't think there's any contradiction there). And they guide people in creating positive change in their own lives and aligning their personal practices with their aspirations for a better world.

And we strive to practice what we preach through what we call "The BK Way." At the core of this approach is *stewardship,* a deep sense of responsibility to administer the company for the benefit of all of our stakeholder groups, including authors, customers, employees, investors, service providers, sales partners, and the communities and environment around us. Everything we do is built around stewardship and our other core values of *quality, partnership, inclusion,* and *sustainability.*

This is why Berrett-Koehler is the first book publishing company to be both a B Corporation (a rigorous certification) and a benefit corporation (a for-profit legal status), which together require us to adhere to the highest standards for corporate, social, and environmental performance. And it is why we have instituted many pioneering practices (which you can learn about at www.bkconnection.com), including the Berrett-Koehler Constitution, the Bill of Rights and Responsibilities for BK Authors, and our unique Author Days.

We are grateful to our readers, authors, and other friends who are supporting our mission. We ask you to share with us examples of how BK publications and resources are making a difference in your lives, organizations, and communities at www.bkconnection.com/impact.

Dear reader,

Thank you for picking up this book and welcome to the worldwide BK community! You're joining a special group of people who have come together to create positive change in their lives, organizations, and communities.

What's BK all about?

Our mission is to connect people and ideas to create a world that works for all.

Why? Our communities, organizations, and lives get bogged down by old paradigms of self-interest, exclusion, hierarchy, and privilege. But we believe that can change. That's why we seek the leading experts on these challenges—and share their actionable ideas with you.

A welcome gift

To help you get started, we'd like to offer you a **free copy** of one of our bestselling ebooks:

www.bkconnection.com/welcome

When you claim your **free ebook**, you'll also be subscribed to our blog.

Our freshest insights

Access the best new tools and ideas for leaders at all levels on our blog at ideas.bkconnection.com.

Sincerely,

Your friends at Berrett-Koehler